Endorsements for *Deathbed Conversions: Finding Faith at the Finish Line*, by Karen Edmisten

I love this book. It has all the attractive power of the supermarket tabloids — big celebrity names, sex, violence, everything but aliens — but with the grace, eloquence, and profundity of Augustine's *Confessions*. It will be the book you most enjoy reading this year.

> — Mike Aquilina, EWTN host and
> author of *The Fathers of the Church*

Lively, engaging stories of conversion that will encourage us to accept the offer of God's friendship in Jesus Christ — and to encourage others to do so — sooner rather than later.

> — The Most Reverend George J. Lucas,
> Archbishop of Omaha

Deathbed Conversions: Finding Faith at the Finish Line is unquestionably a most unique and fascinating book. Author Karen Edmisten has woven compelling and inspiring stories together, which will absolutely stir your heart — you won't be able to put it down!

> — Donna-Marie Cooper O'Boyle, EWTN host and best-selling
> author of sixteen Catholic books, including *Catholic Mom's
> Café: 5-Minute Retreats for Every Day of the Year*

Deathbed
Conversions

FINDING FAITH
at the FINISH LINE

Karen Edmisten

Our Sunday Visitor Publishing Division
Our Sunday Visitor, Inc.
Huntington, Indiana 46750

Dedication

With deepest gratitude to everyone who ever
uttered a prayer for me. And for Heather,
Mauren, Emma, and Kelton.

The Convert

by G.K. Chesterton

After one moment when I bowed my head
And the whole world turned over and came upright,
And I came out where the old road shone white,
I walked the ways and heard what all men said,
Forests of tongues, like autumn leaves unshed,
Being not unlovable but strange and light;
Old riddles and new creeds, not in despite
But softly, as men smile about the dead.

The sages have a hundred maps to give
That trace their crawling cosmos like a tree,
They rattle reason out through many a sieve
That stores the sand and lets the gold go free:
And all these things are less than dust to me
Because my name is Lazarus and I live.

Contents

Chapter 1

Don't Ever Give Up

"I'm looking for loopholes," W.C. Fields supposedly quipped on his deathbed as he flipped through a Bible.

Deathbed conversions sound suspiciously like loopholes, like unfair, unaccounted for, last-minute ducks inside the pearly gates. When he heard that I was writing this book, a relative snorted and asked me, "Do you really believe in those things?" Another friend smirked, shook her head, and said, "Those deathbed conversions aren't fair, y'know."

The thought of a deathbed conversion inspires a host of reactions, usually strong ones. Some people relish the idea of last-minute U-turns. They're heartened by these conversion stories or know someone who knew someone who experienced finish-line contrition. They love to hear about others' spiritual treks, and sigh with satisfaction that lost sheep have been found. After all, an honest-to-goodness deathbed conversion offers everything good storytelling demands: drama, pathos and sin, despair, chaos, confusion, love, enlightenment, and, finally, redemption.

On the other hand, there is the Smirk-and-Snort Contingent. Such skeptics don't believe that genuine conversion occurs late in life. They don't believe people can authentically change, or they suspect duplicitous, mercenary motives. Some chafe at the unfairness factor. Why should the rest of us kill ourselves being "good" all our lives when those lifelong slackers get a final-hour free ticket into heaven? Who let them cut in line anyway?

Living one's entire life without God, though, is hardly a free ticket. A true deathbed convert doesn't rub his hands together at the final hour, snickering, "Hey, I pulled a fast one on the Big Guy!" Rather, he sees the tragedy of a wasted lifetime, the pain of his prolonged denial, and the foolishness of his stubborn *Non Serviam*.

The only glee is the relief and gratitude that God's mercy is offered and poured out to us until the final and bitter end.

Because we can never know what is happening in another person's heart and mind, we don't have an inkling who is quietly seeking God, or how long they may have been doing so. "The heart of another is a dark forest, always," said Willa Cather in her novel *The Professor's House,* "no matter how close it has been to one's own." We can't see for certain when or how someone has begun inching toward Him. We can size up a person's outward actions: we know what is objectively sinful or intrinsically evil. But there's a reason that the Church never definitively answers the question, "Who is in hell?" While the Church does, through the process of canonization, highlight examples of holiness for the faithful to emulate, she never makes a pronouncement about who has been damned. That's because we can't know the state of another person's soul. Let us repeat that: we can't know the state of another person's soul.

Oscar Wilde, one of the subjects of this book, said, "One's real life is so often the life that one does not lead."[1] Real life — our interior, mental, emotional, and spiritual processes — is at the heart of conversion, and at the heart of this book.

The Unseen Other

We've probably all had the jarring experience of discovering a secret about someone we thought we knew. "What?" we sputter, stunned at revelations from the mundane ("You hate Reese's Peanut Butter Cups? No one hates them") to the life-altering ("You could've told me about the baby ... and the adoption ... I would have understood"). Knowing the heart of another is a tricky thing. We spend our lives fumbling through circumstances and relationships that will mold us into the finished products we will become. Every thought and choice, every day, month, and year bring more sharply into focus who we are and what we want to be. Some happy souls stride through life with firm purpose and a grounded identity, and they remain true to that identity their entire lives. I remember one year when I was helping with the RCIA program at my parish. Each team member had been asked to give a witness talk. One sweet woman, the wife of a deacon, was reluctant. I asked her what was wrong. "I don't have a story," she told me shyly. "I've always believed."

"What a gift!" I blurted back. "Do you know that I'd trade you all the drama in my past for what you have? And, by the way, the fact that you 'have no story'? That's your story. Because we all have one, and yours is beautiful."

Sadly, though, we aren't all like that deacon's wife, blessed with a deep, abiding faith from the start. At the other end of the spectrum are the people who grow up in atmospheres of atheism and negativity, or full of anger at the God they insist does not exist. And in between lie stories of every gradation: people who start life with a basic foundation of faith, only to find that they've drifted away without reason, drama, or objections. They've simply floated lazily downriver and don't know how they got there. Others start out with benign unbelief, as I did. We're the sort who were raised in good homes, by good parents — kind people who want to do the right and ethical thing. We had Santa Claus at Christmas and chocolate eggs at Easter. We had nothing against faith in God; we just didn't happen to subscribe to any particular religion.

When we are not in the position of being a friend's most intimate confidante, we can't really know with certitude what that friend thinks, believes, or feels. Even when a friend does confide in us, how can we know for certain that the entirety of the life she is leading is her "real life"?

St. Augustine is famously quoted as saying, "Lord, make me chaste, but not yet." When Augustine made that plea, he sensed what his "real life" — his purpose and calling — was, but he wasn't ready to embrace it yet. I was reminded of his words as I researched the stories in this book. Many converts reach the crossroads at which they desire change, even yearn for it strongly, but "not yet." They want to stand at the fork in the road for a while. I understand that sentiment. Anyone who has experienced longing for God while simultaneously fearing the sacrifices required to follow Him will understand it, too. We would-be converts offer equivocal prayers because although we can comprehend the worthiness of the goal, we can't quite see ourselves crossing that finish line yet. So there's spiritual dawdling, some hemming and hawing. We have to sift through a mountain of "what ifs" and fret over what friends, family, and spouses might say.

But not everyone dawdles, muttering to God, "Umm, could you come back next week? I have a few things I need to take care of first." Some people follow divine promptings right away. They drop everything and run to the Father. Why can't we all be St. Paul on the road to Damascus? I don't know the answer to that question. I know only that every soul is held incalculably dear by our Lord.

It can be tempting for us Christians to resent those who obstinately reject God and then make it all up in the end seemingly on a whim, slipping through that loophole that W.C. Fields tried to find. But authentic deathbed conversions are not the stuff of whims. If they are the genuine acknowledgement that God is God, then they are the final submission to "real life." Rather than resentment, we Christians might discover a host of other feelings when we take a long, hard look: pity for people's squandered lives, compassion for their black holes of despair, sorrow for the chances they missed, and the happiness that could have been theirs had they submitted to God sooner.

As a former atheist and an adult convert, I sympathize with the skepticism of late-life converts and I can relate to their incredulity regarding miracles. I grew up around people who thought of the Bible as a book of fairy tales, and as a young adult my belief system was built around a pragmatic approach to the secular culture. I was an anti-marriage, anti-child, pro-choice know-it-all. But in His infinite mercy, God knocked relentlessly at my door. He sent gifts: patient friends, good books, undeserved grace. He let me hunger and thirst until I finally sought baptism, at the age of thirty, and reception into the Catholic Church five years later.

I have special affection for Scripture passages that address the lost sheep, the prodigal sons, the workers who came late to the vineyard. Obviously mine was hardly a deathbed conversion, coming to Christianity as I did at age thirty, but I know intimately the desire to sweep God away. I didn't want to acknowledge His claim on my life, but I am grateful that for some inexplicable reason I did, long before my deathbed. Having been a Christian now for twenty-two years, and a Catholic for the last seventeen, I can only imagine what the last two decades would have been like had I continued to ignore God's call and persisted in telling Him to come back tomorrow.

I still recall in vivid detail the mixture of pain, fear, relief, and happiness that I felt when I sank to my knees one day, admitting to God and myself the sins I'd committed. I knew the things I'd done were grievous, but I finally understood that He loved and accepted me anyway. Years of desperation could end; I believed there was something else out there for me. I was finally ready to take the leap — and the risk — of faith.

The final, desperate but sincere call for a priest is that same ascent to truth — to the Truth — from which one has been running for a long time. It is at once a mournful moment of recognition that unrecoverable time has been wasted, and at the same time, a giddy celebration: "At last, at last!"

When Does It Get Easy?

Initially, I thought that writing about deathbed conversions would be straightforward. Stories, facts, chronologies — tidy lines framing lives that ended in good deaths. Point A would always lead to Point B. I would merely chronicle the connection of dots, like a statistician relaying the biographical numbers.

It wasn't that easy. As I researched this book, I kept thinking, "The next chapter will be easy but this one is tough … wow, what a life. Who knew?"

Consider Oscar Wilde. I wanted to spend weeks on his story, wanted to have tea with him, to meet him when he was a young man and urge him to ignore what his father had said about the Catholic Church. Then I thought Patricia Neal would be the easy chapter — the Hollywood actress who predictably gets fed up with the glamorous life and gives in to Catholicism. But I discovered such complicating factors as her affair with actor Gary Cooper, her abortion, and her thirty-year marriage to the famous author Roald Dahl.

Dutch Schulz would be a quick glance, though, right? Gangster. Murderer. Afraid of what lies beyond, he calls for a priest in his dying moments. Probably just hedging his bets. And yet how can we claim to know what was going on in the mind of someone who has been a member of organized crime all his life, who has committed ghastly violence, but has begun to glimpse something beyond?

Or consider author, art historian, and creator of the BBC series *Civilisation*, Kenneth Clark. Clark was deeply immersed in worldly concerns when he began to see a connection between the human desire to create and the possibility of a Source from which all beauty flows. And what about the poet Wallace Stevens who spent his life looking for an alternative "something" to believe in when he no longer thought it was possible to believe in God? Would the journalist and Algonquin Round Table regular, Heywood Broun, finally provide me with a simple story, with straight rather than crooked lines? When exactly would I get to the easy part?

> Trying to neatly sum up what happens in the human heart is like trying to wrap your arms around a ray of light.

I was forced to admit defeat because there was no easy part. Conversions don't track in straight lines, and they do not lend themselves to dispassionate reporting. Trying to neatly sum up what happens in the human heart is like trying to wrap your arms around a ray of light. You keep missing; you can't hold on; there's always dust. There was no such thing as an easy chapter in this book because there is no such thing as a simple soul. Every soul has its unique history and deserves its own story. You would think I'd know this, given my own conversion. I have walked my own crooked way. My past, perhaps more than anything, gives me immense compassion for the people in this book. I'm still stumbling, but at least by the grace of God I know now in which direction I want to head. I'm beyond grateful for the mercy that picks me up every day.

Staying the Course

It is worth noting that the conversion stories in this book all share a common feature. The people whose spiritual biographies appear here flatly denied God or hid from the Hound of Heaven for as long as they could, but each had someone in his life who was a beacon of Christ's light. Each had someone who did not give up on him. Christianity is an incarnational faith. Jesus Christ came to us as a human being, and he continues to work with and through flesh and blood, person to person, one soul at a time.

We who sit quietly on the sidelines of the lives of doubters, agnostics, and atheists can take a cue from the families and friends of the converts in these pages. Their example encourages us to never give up on the people we love.

So how do we believers respond to those who are still far from any kind of conversion? What are we to do about the skeptics and atheists in our lives, the people we love, live with, or befriend who don't care about God? The best I can offer is a little bit of my own experience.

I met one of my best friends when I was in high school. I was agnostic-to-atheist, and Jack grew up in a typical, faithfully Mass-attending, Italian-Irish Catholic home. We hit it off in drama class and shared a tendency toward probing discussions about life and the nature of the universe. By the time we were in college, I was a full-fledged, pro-choice atheist, and Jack had fallen away from his Catholic faith and was investigating various other beliefs. His search even took him to a Zen Buddhist monastery in California for a time. Eventually, after years of investigation and prayer, Jack made his way back to the faith in which he'd been raised.

I was another story. Several years after college I was still floundering, cobbling together a philosophy of life from the world around me, and finding it not only unsatisfactory but painful. But when I was a lost sheep, Jack remained a steadfast friend. He knew me through some of the ugliest years of my life. He taught me, sometimes with words, sometimes with simple kindness, that I was more than the sum of my sins. He shared with me the revolutionary notion that my behavior was not the definition of who I was. He told me, and I still remember being struck by how convinced he seemed of this, that one day I would realize that I was worthy of the love that Jesus Christ offered me.

We had endless conversations and countless cups of coffee. We took walks. We had arguments and at other times respectful debates. He prayed. I objected to being prayed for. He prayed anyway. We didn't always discuss religion, though. We were first friends, so we also simply hung out, ate sopapillas, raved about books, dissected movies, went on dates with other people, and talked about whom we had fallen in love with.

Jack sometimes recommended books and magazines to me, things that had been helpful to him on his journey back to the Catholic fold. Sometimes I read them, sometimes I didn't. He explained his faith, but he never pushed it on me.

Eventually, I met and married Tom. Jack got married, too (I was the "best man" at his wedding). Tom and I stayed in touch with Jack and his wife, Holly, even though we moved away. Jack was still available for questions and helped me reconnect with a mutual high school friend who (surprise!) was also happy to answer questions about Christianity. Tentatively, I started to read the Bible. I began to pray, and I asked God to reveal Himself to me if He was there, if He was real.

One day, when I was nearly thirty years old, I invited Jack to an event: my baptism. I had started attending an Episcopal church and was convinced of the need for baptism. Would he come? Yes, he said, he would. Was he disappointed that I hadn't chosen the Catholic Church? (Another Christian friend had responded to my news with a tentative sort of, "Really? The Episcopalians? Can I ask why?" I'd been crushed. I'd thought she would rejoice rather than pick apart my motives, and her reaction was sorely deflating to a fledgling Christian.) But Jack didn't even hint at disappointment. He was elated. He drove five hundred miles to be at the baptism. I had chosen Christ, and he wanted to be there, no matter what Christian denomination it was.

Tom and I moved again, and Jack continued to be my long-distance sounding board and go-to guy for questions about Catholicism, because I still had a lot of questions. He addressed every concern I threw his way about the pope, Mary, the Eucharist, confession, the priesthood, and natural family planning. He recommended more books. It's a safe bet he was still praying for me.

Finally, one day, I invited Jack to another event. Would he drive 120 miles to attend the Easter Vigil Mass at which I was going to be received into the Catholic Church? Yes, he would.

And five years after that? Jack and Holly attended the Mass at which my husband, Tom, was confirmed a Catholic. Jack and Holly are godparents to all of Tom's and my children, and we are all still dear friends.

Friends. My best buddy, the one I sometimes thought was a crazy Jesus freak, acted through all those years out of nothing but love. I am extraordinarily grateful that he never summarily dismissed me simply because I did not share his faith. He had the Christian charity to separate the person I was from the acts I had committed. He understood that the worth of my soul was separate from the evils of which I was guilty. He was, in other words, Christ to me.

In a different, but just as important way, my husband, ironically, was also Christ to me, even before he became a practicing Christian himself. Tom married an atheist girl who swore she would never want children. He didn't bargain for life with a Catholic woman who not only wanted babies, but wanted to introduce natural family planning into the marriage instead of using artificial birth control to help space those babies. He was thrown a disorienting curve ball, to say the least. But he handled it. He stuck with me, worked through the challenges and changes with me, tirelessly forgave me, and loved me unconditionally.

The Lord does not always come to us in recognizable or traditionally "religious" ways. Sometimes the first glimpse many of us see of Jesus Christ is unadorned, all-encompassing love.

It's a little too easy for us Catholics to want to retreat from the world, to hang out only with Catholic friends, with people who understand us and share our values. Make no mistake — there is great merit in finding and nurturing that kind of support. It is not only helpful, but crucial, to cultivate a Catholic culture in our lives, and, more expansively, in our world. At the same time, we are called to be in the world but not of it, and sometimes that means the greatest work of mercy we can perform is to befriend the girl sitting next to us in drama class, or to remain loyal to a wife who has turned our world upside down. God really asks only one thing of us each day — we just have to be Christ to everyone we meet.

No pressure.

I want to strive every day to be the kind of spouse and friend that my husband and friends have been to me. I want to be a beacon, a tiny flicker of the light and possibility of Jesus. I am, simply put, a sinner who's not willing to give up on anyone, because no one gave up on me. When I was twenty years old, mired in grave sin, could my friend have predicted that I would one day become a Catholic? He could have decided that my presence was a stain on his world. Instead, the grace present in his life acted as a conduit that could attract me, draw me in, and become my saving grace, too.

I hope this book can encourage us to strive to be beacons of Christ's light. Instead of shunning those who might taint our hoped-for holiness, we can pray that Christ will shimmer — imperceptibly, perhaps, but strongly — through us.

Never give up on the potential deathbed conversions in your life. If there's a lesson in this book, it's this: it is a grace and a privilege to be the friend who is still around at the end, ready to offer whatever is necessary to help another soul reach for Christ. If we are present at such a genuine moment, we will know without a doubt that a deathbed conversion is not a loophole, or an unfair advantage for the other team. It is the mercy of God at work.

Notes

1. Wilde, Oscar. *Shorter Prose Pieces*. N.p.: Project Gutenberg, 2008. http://www.gutenberg.org/cache/epub/2061/pg2061.html.

CHAPTER 2

King Charles II

May 29, 1630 – February 6, 1685

"Sir, this good man once saved your life. He now
comes to save your soul."[2]
— The Duke of York, to his brother

The twenty-one-year-old man, perched in an oak tree, did his best
to blend with limbs and leaves. It was no mean feat, given his six
foot, two inch frame, but he was highly motivated. Marching below was the young man's enemy in this deadly game of hide and
seek. If General Oliver Cromwell — who had overthrown the English monarchy and established a military dictatorship — glanced
upward and spied young Charles II, the would-be king would be
no more.

It was 1651 and Charles' army had been defeated by Cromwell's a few days earlier at the battle of Worcester. On a mission of
vengeance for his father's beheading, Charles had defied exile and
invaded England in an attempt to regain the crown. Now he was on
the run, a wanted man commanding a handsome bounty.

Charles had fled Worcester and headed to Shropshire. The
Pendrell brothers, five Catholic tenants who worked for the owners
of Boscobel House, were sympathetic to Charles and eager to offer whatever aid they could. The Pendrells cut the king's hair, and
gave him clothes that disguised him as a woodcutter. But the only
shoes they could offer were far too small. Charles walked miles in
the tight, blistering footwear but then, to evade his predators, was
forced to round back to Boscobel. There he joined up with Lord
William Careless, and at least one full day was spent hiding outside

in a downpour. Then came the precarious hours in the tree with Careless supporting him as he slept:

> ... Charles and the colonel stayed the whole day, having taken up with them some bread and cheese and small beer, the colonel having a pillow placed on his knees, that the king might rest his head on it as he sat among the branches.[3]

The Penderells met with Fr. John Huddleston, a Benedictine monk, who suggested that Charles take refuge at Moseley Old Hall where he could safely shelter in a tiny, hidden room known as a priest hole, one of many such rooms carved into Catholic houses beginning with the persecution of Catholics under Elizabeth I. Fr. Huddleston was chaplain at Old Mosely Hall, an estate owned by the Whitgreave family. Once Charles was safely ensconced, Fr. Huddleston tenderly washed and bandaged the fugitive's bloodied feet. Charles read an unpublished booklet written by the priest's uncle, *A Short and Plain Way to the Faith and Church*, and the two men talked. Cromwell's troops again came within inches of the king as he hid, but, finding no evidence of their quarry, finally concluded their search of the house and left.

Thus ended the first meeting between Charles II and the Benedictine monk Huddleston. But it would not be the last.

A Protestant Monarch with Catholic Sympathies

Before we try to follow the winding path of King Charles II's conversion, it might help to take a brief look at the dizzying politics of the era. After the death in 1603 of anti-Catholic Queen Elizabeth of the Tudor Dynasty and the Church of England, the Stuart Dynasty began with Charles' grandfather, James I, followed by James' son, Charles I. Charles I's suppression of Puritanism turned brutal and led to open revolt in Parliament. The English Civil War in 1649 led to the execution of Charles I; Oliver Cromwell established a military dictatorship, and Charles II was exiled. It would be eleven years before King Charles II restored the Stuart dynasty to the throne in 1660. Cromwell had died in 1658, but Charles meant to see justice served to those who had plotted against his father. Nine men were put to death, and he ordered Cromwell's body to be exhumed and reburied in a common grave.

The past now laid to rest, Charles ushered in happier times. His people rejoiced at his return, giddy to be rid of the Puritan Cromwell and eager to fall back on a way of life that embraced parties, dancing, music, and joyous celebrations of Christmas. Charles, good looking, charming, and witty, was known as the Merry Monarch for these reasons, but also for his extracurricular activity: he had at least a dozen illegitimate children with a variety of mistresses. He was seen as religiously tolerant, though some historians called his laissez-faire attitude laziness. His tolerance was not surprising, however, given that his mother, his brother James, his sister-in-law, and his wife, Catherine of Braganza, were all of the Roman persuasion.

Still, it couldn't have been a cake-walk to be a Protestant monarch with Catholic sympathies, and it must have been a challenge for a self-avowed hedonist to consider temperance. Did Charles want to convert earlier in life? Or was he convinced because of political considerations that he could never do so openly? The politics of religion and religion in politics were impossibly intertwined; religious freedom was not exactly a given. What was a monarch to do?

Whatever was happening inwardly, outwardly Charles ruled through tragedies of mammoth proportions. The worst epidemic of plague since the mid-1300s, carried and spread by fleas, hit London in 1665 and claimed an estimated seventy thousand lives. The following year saw the Great Fire of London, which raged for five days and consumed tens of thousands of homes, St. Paul's Cathedral, and dozens of other churches. Charles and his brother, James, Duke of York, joined the firefighting efforts and James even succeeded in creating a firebreak that helped to put an end to the disaster. Charles then had to deal with the rebuilding of London.

All the while, his relationship with Parliament was still rife with conflict. England's laws and culture were deeply anti-Catholic. Charles was Protestant but his tolerance, whether due to progressive thinking, laziness, or political expediency, led to suspicion that he was secretly a Roman Catholic. The fact that he was surrounded by papists did little to allay speculation. Whether for practical, political, or personal considerations, Charles never discussed plans to convert, until one day twelve years into his reign.

Charles struck a deal with his cousin, Louis XIV of France. Louis, attempting to further his ambitions in Europe, sought an alliance with England; the cousins drafted the Treaty of Dover. It declared that France and England would join forces in a war with the Dutch. Louis promised Charles a large amount of cash, which would free Charles from the economic hold of Parliament. That freedom would allow Charles something he now admitted he wanted: conversion to Catholicism. He spoke, too, of beginning to reconcile his country to the Catholic faith. If, Charles decided, his people were not ready to accept this move, he would take Louis XIV up on his promise of more than six thousand troops to speed things along to the desired end.

On the eve of the war in 1672, Charles issued a declaration: all penalties against Catholics were removed. But, in a sudden reversal, he said nothing publicly about his own desire to convert. Perhaps he wanted to hold off until it was more politically feasible. But would it ever be politically feasible?

Parliament refused to release funds for the war with the Dutch until Charles withdrew the declaration. Further, Parliament passed the Test Act, denying all civil and military offices to those who didn't embrace the Anglican Communion and deny the doctrine of transubstantiation. No Catholic could accede to this law. Catholic government officials, including the king's own brother, James, were forced out of government.

Then, in the late 1670s, the English were seized with a kind of mass anti-Catholic hysteria over the "Popish Plot." Ne'er-do-well Titus Oates claimed there was a Jesuit plot to murder the king. There wasn't a shred of truth to the story, but the public sided with Oates. A wave of false accusations sent many Catholics to their deaths. When an accusation of treason was leveled even against

Queen Catherine, Charles sent her out of the country to keep her safe. Then he dissolved Parliament.

He hoped a new Parliament would be more amenable, but it was not to be. Charles and Catherine had not had children, so Charles had no heir, and anti-Catholic factions attempted to exclude his brother James from the line of succession. In response, Charles sent James out of the country and sent the new Parliament home. When they were allowed to reassemble the next year, Parliament struck James from succession, though the action was stopped by the House of Lords. Things became so vitriolic that at one meeting of Parliament both the anti-Catholics and Charles showed up with armed reinforcements. When Parliament attempted to pass yet another Exclusion Act to shut James out, Charles was fed up. He dissolved Parliament and never called another again.

> "The Duke is thinking only of himself. Speak to him. Remind him that there is a soul at stake."

An Unexpected Advocate

With a major source of his misery gone, Charles lived in relative peace for a seventeenth-century king, dodging an assassination plot here, spending considerable time with his mistresses there. Then, in 1685, at the age of fifty-eight, he had a stroke.

It was one of Charles' favorite mistresses, Louise, the Duchess of Portsmouth, who made certain that a priest was called to the king's side in his last hours. James, as heir to the throne, was somewhat preoccupied, to the irritation of the duchess. She pulled the French ambassador aside and insisted that something be done:

> The King is really and truly a Catholic; but he will die without being reconciled to the Church. His bedchamber is full of Protestant clergymen. I cannot enter it without giving scandal. The Duke [James] is thinking only of himself. Speak to him. Remind him that there is a soul at stake. He is master now. He can clear the room. Go this instant, or it will be too late.[4]

The ambassador relayed the message, and James, startled out of the flurry of activity that must occupy a king-to-be, realized he must not let his brother die without receiving the sacraments. But how to accomplish this feat with the king surrounded by Protestants? There was grave danger to any priest who might be called in, as he could be found guilty of a capital offense for receiving someone into the Church. Ideas were discussed and dismissed. Finally

> the Duke commanded the crowd to stand aloof, went to the bed, stooped down, and whispered something that none of the spectators could hear, but which they supposed to be some question about affairs of state. Charles answered in an audible voice, "Yes, yes, with all my heart." None of the bystanders, except the French Ambassador, guessed that the King was declaring his wish to be admitted into the bosom of the Church of Rome.
>
> "Shall I bring a priest?" said the Duke. "Do, brother," replied the sick man. "For God's sake do, and lose no time. But no; you will get into trouble."
>
> "If it costs me my life," said the Duke, "I will fetch a priest."[5]

Someone then remembered that Fr. Huddleston, Charles' companion years before in the Moseley Hall priest hole, and who had become a privileged friend of the court, was currently at Whitehall Palace. The room was cleared, and Huddleston, disguised in a cloak and a wig, was brought to the king by way of a back staircase. "Sir," said the Duke, "this good man once saved your life. He now comes to save your soul."[6] The priest heard Charles' confession and administered last rites. He asked the king if he wanted to receive the Eucharist.

> "Surely," Charles replied, "if I am not unworthy."
>
> The host was brought in. Charles feebly strove to rise and kneel before it. The priest made him lie still and assured

him that God would accept the humiliation of the soul, and would not require the humiliation of the body....

During the night, Charles earnestly recommended the Duchess of Portsmouth and her boy to the care of James; "And do not," he good-naturedly added, "let poor Nelly [his other favored mistress] starve."[7]

Charles' wife, Catherine, had kept vigil at his side for as long as she could manage. Finally, upon seeing her husband in great pain, she had fainted and was carried to bed.

The Queen sent excuses for her absence by Halifax. She said that she was too much disordered to resume her post by the couch, and implored pardon for any offense that she might unwittingly have given. "She asks my pardon, poor woman!" cried Charles; "I ask hers with all my heart."[8]

In his final moments, Charles displayed to those surrounding him the charm that, despite his mistakes as a monarch, made a lasting impression on and inspired affection in nearly all he met. He apologized to everyone for the trouble he had been causing all night. He had been, he said, "a most unconscionable time dying," but he "hoped that they would excuse it."

On February 6, 1685, the Merry Monarch died, a Catholic at last.

Notes

2. Babington Macaulay, Thomas. *The History of England from the Accession of James II*. Vol. I. N.p.: Project Gutenberg, 2008. http://www.gutenberg.org/files/1468/1468-h/1468-h.htm.
3. Ibid.
4. Ibid.
5. Ibid.
6. Ibid.
7. Ibid.
8. Ibid.

CHAPTER 3

Oscar Wilde

October 16, 1854 – November 30, 1900

"My courtiers called me the Happy Prince, and happy
indeed I was, if pleasure be happiness."[9]
— Oscar Wilde

If you know only one thing about Oscar Wilde, it is likely one
of the following: he wrote *The Importance of Being Earnest.* He
quipped, "I can resist everything except temptation."[10] He was a
flamboyant, homosexual dandy. He wielded a razor-sharp wit. "I
am so clever," he said, "that sometimes I don't understand a single
word of what I am saying."[11]

His friends and followers may or may not have understood
him, but they unquestionably loved and celebrated him. Wilde
was an intellectual powerhouse, a wit, a gifted poet, and a playwright. He had a robust social life that could, at least superficially,
be summed up in words from one of his stories: "I like persons better than principles, and I like persons with no principles better than
anything else in the world."[12]

This vision of Oscar Wilde — the happily unrestrained hedonist who once told a customs agent that he had nothing to de-
clare but his genius — is a common one. But there was infinitely
more to this fascinating and complicated man who also once said
that Catholicism was the only religion worth dying in. He had a
lifelong romantic dalliance with the Catholic Church, and he finally succumbed to her as he lay dying.

In "*De Profundis,*" a letter Wilde wrote while in prison, he
said that he hoped to reach a point at which he could simply say
that the greatest turning points in his life were when his father sent

him to Oxford and society sent him to prison. With characteristi-
cally keen insight, Wilde targeted precisely the events that shaped
who and what he was. Both his time at Oxford and his years in prison reverberated through all that followed. If Oxford was the making of the man, prison — while it most assuredly appeared to his
contemporaries to be his undoing — was the remaking. How did
this brilliant Oxford student, successful novelist, and playwright
land in prison, and how did these two turning points define the
elusive Oscar Wilde?

To Eat from Every Tree

In 1854, Oscar Fingal O'Flahertie Wills Wilde was born in Dublin,
Ireland, to Jane and Sir William Wilde, a pair not without their
own fascinating, complicated personalities, accomplishments, and
notoriety. Jane was a poet, linguist, political activist, and a sup-
porter of women's rights who once called for armed revolution in
Ireland. William, a prominent physician, had three illegitimate
children before he married Jane, and was also a gifted writer who
penned several works on medicine, archaeology, and Irish folklore.
Knighted for his work in the medical field, he later fell from public
grace when he was obliquely accused of sexual assault. What really
happened was never entirely clear, but the whole affair was sordid
and neither of Oscar's parents emerged from it pristine. Ward and
June Cleaver they were not.

What did ten-year-old Oscar make of such scandal in his
parents' lives? We can't know for sure, but one assumes the effect
on a child was not a wholesome one. Perhaps Oscar Wilde could
have added a third bullet point to his list of life-changing events: his
birth into this eccentric family. He did, however, love his mother
dearly and grew up on good terms with her, eager to please. His
relationship with his father, on the other hand, was always difficult
for this sensitive young man.

Both peers and biographers have speculated that Wilde
might have converted to Catholicism earlier in life if his father

hadn't been so vehemently opposed to the Church, threatening to cut him off financially should Wilde do the unthinkable. Wilde himself once remarked to a friend, "I am sure that if I had become a Catholic at that time he would have cast me off altogether. Seeing me 'on the brink,' he struck me out of his will. It was a terrible disappointment to me. I suffer a great deal from my Romish leanings, in pocket and mind."[13]

Those Romish leanings first bloomed in Oxford. Wilde landed there at the age of twenty, after three years of study at Trinity College. He swiftly established himself at Oxford as an excellent student who was witty, charming, artistic, sensitive to and interested in beauty, and intrigued by the Catholic faith of his friends. He read the works of Cardinal John Henry Newman, and came within inches of being baptized, but in the end stood up the priest and ducked out on his appointment.

Strongly influenced by one of his Oxford tutors, English writer and critic Walter Pater, Wilde soon became a follower of aestheticism, a literary and artistic movement (sometimes summarized as "art for art's sake") and a leader in aestheticism's sister, literary decadence. But there was more to the philosophy, according to Pater, who expounded on his ideas in his book *Studies in the History of the Renaissance*. Beyond merely advocating for the elevation of beauty and free expression in art, Pater argued that the meaning of life itself was found in seeking new and intense experiences. Much later, Wilde described Pater's book as the one that "... had such a strange influence over my life."[14] Wilde and his fellow aesthetes, while emphasizing pleasure and sensory experience, denied that art must have any underlying moral foundation or compass.

After Oxford, Wilde became a successful writer in short order, winning prestigious prizes, publishing poetry, lecturing in the U.S., Canada, England and Ireland, and writing plays, essays, and fairy tales. At age thirty, Wilde married and quickly had two sons with his wife Constance, but the marriage was surely doomed; one of the intense sensory experiences Wilde regularly sought was homosexual activity.

Extremely telling are the parallels between Wilde's life and his only novel, *The Picture of Dorian Gray*, which was published in 1891. Written some ten years before Wilde's conversion and death, Dorian Gray offers a portrait of hedonism, selfish desires, rampant but well-hidden sin, and the decay of a soul consumed by its own appetites.

Dorian is a beautiful young man who is powerfully influenced and seduced by an older, more experienced man of the world. Lord Henry manipulates Dorian by introducing him to a book that is, Dorian thinks, "poisonous" but mesmerizing.

> "That book you sent me so fascinated me that I forgot how the time was going," Dorian tells Lord Henry.
>
> "Yes, I thought you would like it," replied his host, rising from his chair.
>
> "I didn't say I liked it, Harry. I said it fascinated me. There is a great difference."
>
> "Ah, you have discovered that?" murmured Lord Henry.[15]

Dorian is repulsed by the book but inexplicably attracted. In a strange sort of "prayer" desperately uttered after Lord Henry has awakened new desires and vanities, Dorian wishes that he could remain forever young in appearance, while a recently painted portrait of him could suffer the ravages of age. Dorian then descends into a life of utter selfishness, constant pleasure-seeking, drugs, and ultimately violence and murder. It's a frightening and accurate portrayal of a slow but steady slide into sin and evil. What is at first strange, forbidden, and darkly tantalizing to Dorian becomes a way of life, a sensual pleasure, and an addiction.

The portrait, hidden in Dorian's home, takes on more than mere wrinkles and thinning hair. It becomes something foul, decayed and corrupted by the weight of Dorian's sins. Ultimately, he cannot bear to be in its presence, so he vows to destroy this mute, accusing conscience — the witness to his depravity and a vulgar display of the state of his soul. When he slashes the painting through with a knife, the painting is then restored to its original, innocent beauty. The hideous corruption it had borne is transferred back to Dorian's body. Dorian dies — twisted, ugly, and disfigured by years of self-indulgence.

Perhaps Oscar Wilde's immersion into aestheticism and decadence, and the years that followed his Oxford transformation, were of a similar stripe. Did an atmosphere at Oxford lead Oscar Wilde to become both a Dorian Gray and a Lord Henry? Wilde himself wrote in a letter, "Basil Hallward [the artist who painted Dorian's portrait] is what I think I am: Lord Henry is what the world thinks me: Dorian is what I would like to be — in other ages, perhaps."[16] Did his quest for the next passionate, sensory experience plunge him into a life that he ultimately hated or that led him to hate himself? Wilde addressed the idea this way:

> I remember when I was at Oxford saying to one of my friends as we were strolling round Magdalen's narrow bird-haunted walks one morning in the year before I took my degree, that I wanted to eat of the fruit of all the trees in the garden of the world, and that I was going out into the world with that passion in my soul.[17]

Doing Time

Though Oscar and his wife, Constance, never divorced even through Oscar's infidelities, Constance did change her sons' surnames following the worst scandal of Oscar's life. In 1895, Wilde became a convicted felon.

His own hubris was at least partly to blame. Oscar was involved with a man named Lord Alfred Douglas, whose nickname was Bosie. Bosie was the son of the Marquess of Queensberry, who strongly objected to the relationship between Oscar and Bosie. He publicly accused Oscar of sodomy, an incident that might have played out differently if Wilde had not charged Queensberry with libel. In proving himself innocent of libel, Queensberry succeeded in getting Oscar arrested and convicted on charges of gross indecency. Wilde was sentenced to two years of hard labor in prison.

The time in jail — that second great turning point in Oscar Wilde's life — proved profound. Incarcerated and alone, he looked inward. He returned to reading Cardinal Newman; he read St. Augustine and Dante; he read the Gospels. He contemplated suffering — his own and the idea of it. He wrote *"De Profundis,"* the title (Latin for "from the depths") of which is a reference to Psalm 130: "Out of the depths I cry to thee, O Lord! Lord, hear my voice!" Often referred to as an essay, *"De Profundis"* was actually a letter written to Bosie, recounting the rumination and growth Wilde was experiencing. As he reflected on his past actions and current sufferings, the blur that was his life seemed to swim into focus. He still did not denounce his choices to pursue pleasure at all costs (and was still three years away from his deathbed and final request for conversion) but another perspective was dawning on him — that particular roads traveled led to sufferings that, perhaps, had befallen him for a reason. He wrote:

> Those whom he [Christ] saved from their sins are saved simply for beautiful moments in their lives.... All that Christ says to us by the way of a little warning is that every moment should be beautiful, that the soul should always be ready for the coming of the bridegroom.[18]

This was not the first time that threads of Christianity were woven into Wilde's contemplation. Fairy tales published in the late 1880s showed explicitly Christian themes. *The Happy Prince* and *The Selfish Giant* are delicate stories of love and sacrifice and are evidence, partnered with his longtime fascination with the ritual and beauty of the Catholic Church, that Wilde was not always or only the acerbic cynic he appeared to be. His poem "The Ballad of Reading Gaol" (which was written two years after his release from prison and recounts the execution, which Wilde witnessed, of a murderer) displays a sensitivity to the kind of suffering that is often a precursor to conversion:

> Ah! happy they whose hearts can break
> And peace of pardon win!
> How else may man make straight his plan

And cleanse his soul from Sin?
How else but through a broken heart
May Lord Christ enter in?[19]

Perhaps Wilde's observation that "one's real life is so often the life that one does not lead" offers one of the most accurate clues to the authentic Oscar Wilde. His interior life was clearly complex and layered. Did he spend decades hiding behind a facade of wit and sensual pleasure, only to be inwardly questioning, wondering, even yearning for Jesus Christ, who was, in Wilde's words, "just like a work of art"? "*De Profundis*" certainly seems to point to such longing.

Washed Up in Paris

Upon his release from prison, Oscar's first wish was to attend a six-month long retreat with the Jesuits. What an astounding request! Surely they embraced this broken man and helped him to fully realize conversion. No. Heartbreakingly, his request was denied. It's hard to believe that the rejection didn't crush what must have become a deep, gnawing hope for redemption, mercy, and charity. "Every saint has a past, and every sinner has a future,"[20] Oscar once said, but perhaps he no longer believed in a future with the Catholic Church after being abandoned so coldly.

> "Every saint has a past, and every sinner has a future."

The final three years of Wilde's life were painful and sad. He had no money, no social standing, and only a handful of friends as he lay dying in an ugly, cheap hotel room in Paris. But even near the end, this amalgamation of battling sensibilities couldn't resist a quip. He purportedly said to a friend, "My wallpaper and I are fighting a duel to the death. One or the other of us has to go."[21]

The cause of his death was long speculated to be syphilis, but recent study points to complications from an ear infection that had moved to his brain. In his final days, Wilde's longtime and still loyal friend Robbie Ross, a convert to Catholicism, called a priest. Fr. Cuthbert Dunne recalled that he was asked to "come in haste to attend a dying man." Fr. Dunne said he firmly believed Wilde knew exactly what he was doing:

> He could be roused and was roused from this state in my presence. When roused, he gave signs of being inwardly conscious. He made brave efforts to speak, and would even continue for a time trying to talk, though he could not utter articulate words. Indeed, I was fully satisfied that he understood me when told that I was about to receive him into the Catholic Church and give him the last sacraments. From the signs he gave, as well as from his attempted words, I was satisfied as to his full consent. And when I repeated close to his ear the Holy Names, the Acts of Contrition, Faith, Hope, and Charity, with acts of humble resignation to the Will of God, he tried all through to say the words after me.[22]

Wilde died on November 30, 1900.

> "Bring me the two most precious things in the city," said God to one of His Angels; and the Angel brought Him the leaden heart (of the prince) and the dead bird. "You have rightly chosen," said God, "for in my garden of Paradise this little bird shall sing for evermore, and in my city of gold the Happy Prince shall praise me."
>
> — "The Happy Prince"[23]

Notes

9. Wilde, Oscar. *The Happy Prince and Other Tales*. N.p.: Project Gutenberg, 2009. http://www.gutenberg.org/files/30120/30120-h/30120-h.htm.

10. Wilde, Oscar. *Lady Windermere's Fan*. N.p.: Project Gutenberg, 1997. http://www.gutenberg.org/dirs/etext97/lwfan10h.htm.

11. Wilde, Oscar. *The Happy Prince and Other Tales*. N.p.: Project Gutenberg, 2009. http://www.gutenberg.org/files/30120/30120-h/30120-h.htm.

12. Wilde, Oscar. *The Picture of Dorian Gray*. N.p.: Project Gutenberg, 2008. http://www.gutenberg.org/files/174/174-h/174-h.htm.
13. "Wilde's Romish Leanings." *Catholic Herald UK*, November 20, 2009. http://archive.catholicherald.co.uk/article/20th-november-2009/7/wildes-romish-leanings.
14. Wilde, Oscar. *De Profundis*. N.p.: Project Gutenberg, 2007. http://www.gutenberg.org/files/921/921-h/921-h.htm.
15. Wilde, Oscar. *The Picture of Dorian Gray*. N.p.: Project Gutenberg, 2008. http://www.gutenberg.org/files/174/174-h/174-h.htm.
16. Dawson, Terence. "Dorian Gray as Symbolic Representation of Wilde's Personality." The Victorian Web. http://www.victorianweb.org/authors/wilde/dawson16.html.
17. Wilde, Oscar. *De Profundis*. N.p.: Project Gutenberg, 2007. http://www.gutenberg.org/files/921/921-h/921-h.htm.
18. Ibid.
19. Wilde, Oscar. *The Ballad of Reading Gaol*. N.p.: Project Gutenberg, 2008. http://www.gutenberg.org/files/301/301-h/301-h.htm.
20. Wilde, Oscar. *A Woman of No Importance*. N.p.: Project Gutenberg, 1997. http://www.gutenberg.org/cache/epub/854/pg854.html.
21. A photo, taken by a friend, of Wilde on his deathbed next to the notorious wallpaper can be found in *A Certain Genius*, by Barbara Belford.
22. Burke, C.P., Rev. Edmund. "Oscar Wilde: The Final Scene." *The London Magazine*, May 1961 http://www.poetrymagazines.org.uk/magazine/record.asp?id=9404.
23. Wilde, Oscar. *The Happy Prince and Other Tales*. N.p.: Project Gutenberg, 2009. http://www.gutenberg.org/files/30120/30120-h/30120-h.htm.

CHAPTER 4

Buffalo Bill
(William Frederick Cody)
February 26, 1846 – January 10, 1917

"And it's in my old age I have found God — and I realize how easy it is to abandon sin and serve Him."[24]
— William Cody

The April 20, 1876, telegram relayed an urgent message. Bill Cody, who was appearing in a play based on his adventures as a buffalo hunter and scout, was informed that his five-year-old son, Kit Carson Cody, was seriously ill. Scarlet fever. Bill couldn't get a train out of Springfield, Massachusetts, into Rochester, New York, until nine o'clock p.m., so he finished the first act of the play, raced to the train station, and worried through the agonizing journey home. When he arrived, "Kitty" was in grave condition. He died that night.

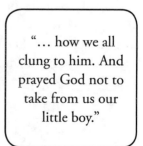

"… how we all clung to him. And prayed God not to take from us our little boy."

Two days later, Cody wrote to his sister, Julia, that God "sent the angel of death to take the treasure that he had given us five years and five months ago. And how dear he had grown to us in that time. And when we seen that there was danger of him leaving us how we all clung to him. And prayed God not to take from us our little boy."[25]

Cody was crushed by the loss. Six weeks later, he bowed out of the play to accept a job once again as an army scout, this time for General George Crook. Cody would revisit both a life in the theater and the death of a beloved child, but for now he was reprising his role as a player in the Indian wars.

A Legend, a Hero — and Human

Buffalo Bill's name evokes glittering images beyond the humdrum
of reality: acclaimed folk hero, dazzling entertainer, spellbinding
storyteller, rugged hunter, daring Union scout and guide in the
Civil War, Western Renaissance man, and both caricature and idealization of the American cowboy. He was a charmer with a hearty
sense of humor who, despite his early reputation as an "Indian
fighter," was a fair-minded man who later supported the rights of
Native Americans.

Not only did he believe in women's suffrage, he said women
should have "even more liberty than they have and do any kind of
work they see fit."[26] A believer in equal-pay-for-equal-work, Cody
paid sharpshooter Annie Oakley the same wages he paid the men in
his Wild West show. The nation's most renowned bison hunter, he,
in the end, championed conservation of the species.

He was myth, legend, tall tale, hero.

The loss of his father, Isaac, when Will Cody was just eleven years old, was perhaps the birth of the determined young man
who would become Buffalo Bill. Toughness and bravery weren't
options; they were tools for survival as he stepped up to help support his family. But life-or-death challenges meshed well with the
boy's innate sense of adventure. Always on the lookout for the next
thrill ride, Will got a job with the Pony Express when he was just
fourteen. "Mail carrier" may not conjure glamorous images in the
twenty-first century, but in 1860 a high-speed relay race on horseback was this boy's idea of fun. At eighteen, he fought in the Civil
War and went on to work as a scout for the U.S. Army. His job as
bison hunter for the railroad, providing food for workers, earned
him his famous nickname. In an autobiography, he joked that the
name was not a compliment:

> When the men would see me coming with a load of fresh
> meat they would say: "Ah, here comes Bill with a lot of nice

buffalo." For a while they were delighted with the fresh, tender meat, but after a time they tired of it, and, seeing me come, would say: "Here comes this old Bill with more buffalo!"[27]

His adventures later led him to unexpected career turns. He became the subject of pot-boiling, dashed-off dime novels, and the star of a show that toured the world and endured for thirty years. He led foreign dignitaries such as the Grand Duke Alexis of Russia on hunting parties. In 1872, he received the Congressional Medal of Honor for valor, one of just four civilians at the time to receive the award.

But behind the shimmering facade of his life story, William Frederick Cody was not above or beyond reality. He made mistakes, slogged through failure, and endured his share of unhappiness. The hero was human.

When he was nineteen, Will met Louisa Frederici. Her cousin, Will McDonald, told her he planned to bring a friend over, a dashing young soldier he was sure she'd like. Louisa had dozed off in front of the fireplace while waiting for her guests' arrival, and when she suddenly felt her chair being swept out from under her, she reached up to slap her cousin for his impertinent prank.

I whirled angrily, and my right hand sped through the air. "Will McDonald!" I cried as I felt my hand strike flesh, "if you ever do that again, I'll...." Then I stopped and blushed and stammered. For I had slapped, full in the mouth, a young man I never before had seen! The young man rubbed his lips ruefully, eyed me for a second, then began to laugh. My cousin, doubled over with joy at the unexpected success of his joke, at last managed to choke out the words: "Louisa, this is the young man I told you about. Allow me to present Private William Frederick Cody of the United States Army."[28]

It was an ironic foreshadowing of what would become a troubled marriage between two stubborn combatants. Will and Louisa, also known as Lulu, had four children, Arta, Kit Carson,

Orra, and Irma. They suffered the losses of two of their children: Kit in 1876, and eleven-year-old Orra in 1883. The couple fought constantly about money (how to spend it when they had it, who was to blame when they did not), alcohol (Bill had a strong affection for strong drink), and the pretty women in Cody's shows. Several separations and a divorce suit were in their future. At the divorce hearing, Cody claimed he'd been tricked into marriage, though the evidence indicates that he knew exactly what he was doing — and in fact Bill and Lulu remained married until Cody died.

Doing Right

When he was struggling to support his growing family, Cody met Ned Buntline, a dime novelist who saw in Buffalo Bill the perfect protagonist for books and show biz. Buntline wrote a serial story based loosely on Cody's exploits, and the western adventurer became a national celebrity. When the stories were adapted for the stage, Buffalo Bill added "actor" to his resume. His show — "Buffalo Bill's Wild West" — toured the country and Europe, making him a star and a wealthy man.

Generous to a fault, Cody shared his fortune with his sisters, bestowed loans (which he never expected to be repaid) on old friends, and carried a supply of silver dollars that he doled out freely to anyone who wanted one. He invested in hotels, ranches, mines, and even dabbled in film making. Some of his ideas met with stunning success: in 1895 he helped found Cody, Wyoming, and a few years later, he built the Irma Hotel (named after his daughter), which still operates today. Fr. George Beecher, an Episcopal priest who knew Cody during the years of the Wild West, knew him as a loyal and honest man who helped to build a number of churches. Bill was also behind the *Cody Enterprise*, a newspaper still running in the town after which it is named. Other gambles, such as "Yosemite Yarrow Cough Cream," and "Panamalt," a drink purported to substitute for both coffee and alcohol, failed to find a market.

The charismatic entertainer, entrepreneur, and philanthropist who embodied the American Dream was perhaps the most famous man on the planet by the year 1900 and a friend to all, from the artist Frederick Remington to presidents and children. Once, when his cousin, a social worker in New York City, wrote asking if she could bring a group of underprivileged boys to the Wild West show, Cody sent her a ticket admitting as many as she wished, and said, "I love children, bring them all."[29]

Buffalo Bill's astounding success and entrepreneurial spirit would not, however, carry him through his final years. The Wild West show eventually began to lose its luster and money, and poor investments drained Cody's bank account. In the face of vague but growing health problems he kept the show going far longer than he wished as he desperately tried to earn enough money on which to retire.

In late 1916, while visiting his sister, Cody was exhausted from the strain of the show and caught a cold, which threatened to turn serious. Lulu and Irma quickly joined him in Denver, fearful he could no longer hold up under the stress and anxiety of working. But he rallied, promising to follow his doctor's orders to quit smoking. Then in January 1917, while trying to get some much-needed rest in Glenwood Springs, he collapsed and was taken back to Denver. On January 8 came a public announcement that Buffalo Bill was dying, and on January 9 Fr. Christopher Walsh was called in from the Cathedral of the Immaculate Conception to baptize Cody and receive him into the Catholic Church. His connection to Fr. Walsh is unclear.

There is speculation that his baptism was at his wife's request, but Cody had come to God on his own terms. In a 1905 letter to his sister, Cody had written

And it's in my old age I have found God — and I realize how easy it is to abandon sin and serve Him. When one stops to think how little they have to give up to serve God, it's a wonder so many more don't do it. A person only has to do right. Through this knowledge I have quit drinking entirely. And quit doing rash things simply by controlling my passions and temper when I find myself getting angry.[30]

William Frederick Cody died of kidney failure on January 10, 1917.

Notes

24. Buffalo Bill Historical Center. "Letter from William F. Cody to sister Julia Goodman." http://library.bbhc.org/cdm/compoundobject/collection/BBOA/id/400/rec/1.

25. Buffalo Bill's Great Plains. "Letter from William F. Cody to Julia Cody Goodman." http://spacely.unl.edu/buffalobill/items/show/107.

26. Wikipedia. "Buffalo Bill." http://en.wikipedia.org/wiki/Buffalo_Bill#cite_ref-42.

27. Cody, William F. *True Tales of the Plains*. N.p.: Archive.org, 2007. http://archive.org/stream/truetalesplains00billgoog/truetalesplains-00billgoog_djvu.txt.

28. Frederici Cody, Louisa. *Memories of Buffalo Bill*. N.p.: Archive.org, 2008. http://www.archive.org/stream/memoriesofbuffal00codyrich#page/2/mode/2up.

29. Russell, Don. *The Lives and Legends of Buffalo Bill*. Norman: University of Oklahoma Press, 1960, 438.

30. Buffalo Bill Historical Center . "Letter from William F. Cody to sister Julia Goodman." 1960. http://library.bbhc.org/cdm/compoundobject/collection/BBOA/id/400/rec/1.

CHAPTER 5

Dutch Schultz

(Arthur Flegenheimer)

August 6, 1902 – October 24, 1935

"Mother is the best bet, and don't let Satan draw you too fast."[31]

— Last words of Dutch Schultz

He apologized for it.

"Dick, you must hate me for this," Arthur Flegenheimer, a.k.a. Dutch Schultz, said to his lawyer, Richard "Dixie" Davis, after Davis witnessed the murder.[32] Davis, in the benign role of delivery man, had deposited Jules Martin, a restaurant rackets thug, at the Harmony Hotel to discuss a financial matter with the boss. More than $70,000 had gone missing, and Schultz was sure Martin had stolen the money. When Martin denied the $70,000 but admitted to pilfering about a third of that amount, Schultz swiftly stuck a gun in the transgressor's mouth and pulled the trigger. He apologized to Davis and told him he could leave. When Davis later read in the paper that Martin's body was found in a snowbank, he was shocked to read that the man had been stabbed a dozen times in the chest. He asked Dutch what happened after the shooting.

"I cut his heart out," Schultz replied as nonchalantly as if he were recounting a stop at the drycleaners.[33]

Schultz, also known as the Beer Baron, did whatever he had to do to keep his business ventures running smoothly. Once, Schultz cut into the territory of a pair of bootlegging brothers. John and Joe Rock did not initially back down, but when John saw Schultz was a serious threat to his personal wellbeing, he backed off. Joe was not as quick to give up his market share. Schultz and his gang kidnapped Joe Rock, beat him, hung him by his thumbs on a meathook then blindfolded him with an infection-soaked bandage that destroyed his eyesight. As if torture wasn't enough, Rock's family allegedly had to pay a $35,000 ransom to get him back.

But Dutch had his own self-prescribed set of ethical standards. There were two areas of crime that Flegenheimer never touched: prostitution and drugs. One night at the Sewanee Club a reporter asked Schultz about his association with "Waxey" Gordon and "Chink" Sherman, two gangsters who were well known for trafficking in human goods and misery. Schultz responded with the sincerity that perhaps only a principled gangster can perfect, "I may do a lot of lousy things, but I'll never make a living off women or narcotics."[34] Dutch had no problem patronizing ladies of the night, but he didn't believe in using them as commodities for his own financial gain.

And his financial gain was considerable. Dutch Schultz was a mobster, bootlegger, gambler, extortionist, killer, and at one time "Public Enemy Number One." The story of his life unfolds like a Saturday matinee featuring every gangster you've ever heard of. Among his contemporaries, friends, and enemies, were Lucky Luciano, Meyer Lansky, Bugsy Siegel, Legs Diamond, Mad Dog Coll, and various other racketeers who ran an operation that came to be known as Murder, Inc. With this lineup, you can practically hear the rapid fire, Cagney-esque conversation, picture the snub-nosed .38s, and see hard-as-nails dames dressed in blood-red dresses, dragging on cigarettes and getting slapped around in the background. But Schultz's life was no gangster movie from which one can emerge into the sunlight, leaving the ugliness behind. The tough stuff was real from the start for Dutch Schultz.

The Making of a Public Enemy

Arthur Flegenheimer was born in 1902 to German-Jewish immigrants in New York. Parents Herman and Emma did not, however, practice their faith and Schultz later claimed he had never seen the inside of a synagogue. Herman abandoned the family when his son was a boy, either eight years old, or fourteen, depending on the source. Young Flegenheimer himself was not a reliable source for such facts. He told conflicting stories about his father, never acknowledging abandonment. He usually said his father had died when he was fourteen, then cut questioners off and changed the subject.

Arthur went to work to help support his family but quickly stumbled onto criminal means to obtain that support. He was arrested for the first time at age seventeen for unlawful entry, and over the years there would be twelve more arrests for increasingly serious and vicious crimes. Even his name was stolen — he lifted it from the son of his employer at Schultz Trucking. Eventually Dutch got into the liquor business at a time when that line of work was both illegal and lucrative.

Schultz partnered with an old friend named Joey Noe and they prospered handsomely from their string of speakeasies. The partnership lasted as long as Noe did. In October of 1928, Noe was shot outside a club on West 54th Street, probably by rival gang members. Though he was wearing a bulletproof vest, shots to Noe's chest, spine, and hand left him mortally wounded, and he died almost a month later. Schultz was furious. He grieved the death of his friend, the only man who had continued to call him Arthur after he'd become "the Dutchman," and the only friend he took along on visits home to his mother.

Noe was the best friend Dutch had ever had, and business had been great under their partnership. But after Noe was killed, Schultz inherited the whole thing. With Dutch as sole proprietor, the enterprise thrived even more and the Beer Baron of the Bronx was flush with success.

In addition to his talents as a beer runner, Dutch was handy with the Harlem numbers racket and other forms of gambling, extortion, tax evasion, and various nefarious money-making schemes. His lucrative career ended abruptly one night at a Newark, New Jersey, restaurant unglamorously named the Palace Chop House.

Here's what led up to the events of that night. Schultz had become something of a loose cannon in the underworld. He made no secret of his plan to kill the New York County special prosecutor, Thomas Dewey. Dewey was famous for his efforts at fighting organized crime, and he'd given Schultz plenty of trouble over the years. Schultz said — frequently and ill-advisedly — "Dewey's gotta go." His indiscreet proclamations were drawing undue attention to business matters that needed to stay a bit more undercover. Dutch's colleagues, including Lucky Luciano, were fed up with Schultz's careless mouthing off, and they decided that Dutch was the one who's "gotta go."

Charlie "The Bug" Workman and Emmanuel "Mendy" Weiss were handed the assignment. They entered the Palace Chop House on October 23, 1935, expecting to find Dutch at his usual table, facing the front door. They were surprised. He wasn't sitting there. They opened fire on the men they did find seated, three of Schultz's associates, including Bernard "Lulu" Rosencrantz, who was shot seven times. Then they went hunting for their chief target. Dutch had no idea the hit was coming and had headed to the bathroom just moments before the assassins arrived. He was caught rather indelicately off guard at the urinal when Workman and Weiss found him. They shot him (using rusty bullets that would cause infection, just in case the shots alone didn't do the trick) and fled.

Schultz dragged himself out of the bathroom, staggered to a table, sank into a chair, and asked for a doctor. Rosencrantz, fighting for his life, threw a quarter at the bartender, asked for change, made it to the phone booth, and called the operator before he passed out.

The police arrived and found the blood-covered Schultz slumped in a chair. They asked who had shot him. Dutch said he didn't know. An ambulance arrived, collected Dutch, and took him to the hospital.

Preposterous — Or Not?

At Newark City Hospital, Schultz asked for a priest. Stories vary as to just how Dutch Schultz and Fr. Cornelius McInerney had originally met. Fr. McInerney was the chaplain at the Hudson County jail when Schultz had had a short stay there. The only thing Schultz said about his relationship with Fr. McInerney was that he knew and admired him for his work against the Ku Klux Klan's anti-Catholic bigotry. However they'd met, and despite the fact that he had indicated he was Jewish when he entered the hospital, Schultz requested the priest's presence. Fr. McInerney arrived, talked with Schultz, baptized him, and administered last rites. When confused reporters asked the cleric why he was there, he stated simply that Schultz had called him. The mortally wounded man, Fr. McInerney said, wanted to die a Catholic.

Suffering from peritonitis, Schultz raved nonsense through his 106 degree fever in his final hours. His last words have been transcribed, analyzed, and even turned into a script, though there is little in them that makes sense. "Mother is the best bet, and don't let Satan draw you too fast," he said, and, "The Chimney Sweeps. Talk to the Sword. Shut up, you got a big mouth!... French Canadian bean soup.... I want to pay, let them leave me alone...."[35]

The next day, Schultz died. He received a Catholic funeral and was buried in Gate of Heaven Catholic cemetery. There was an outcry over this from various quarters. Many found it scandalous that such a vicious man, clearly guilty of countless despicable crimes, could be so easily "accepted" by the Catholic Church.

But Fr. John Toomey, S.J., addressed the issue eloquently in an article in *America* magazine in 1935. His words pierce the heart of conversion, illuminating God's mercy.

> Here was the Catholic Church ... beckoning into her fold a man who through his entire life had represented everything that the Church abhorred and condemned.... "Dutch Schultz" associating with the holy saints in heaven! He to get the same reward as valiant souls who have clung to the Faith through a ceaseless hurricane of trial and temptation. It seemed more than unjust. It seemed ridiculous, preposterous, almost laughable.

But it may not be so laughable after all. There were a number of things not taken into account by the … judges. One little thing they missed completely was the fact that there is just One in the entire universe Who is capable of accurately judging the complex skein of a man's life. The influence of bad example, of environment in general: of heredity; the lack of religious training; the exact strength of temptations…. That One is God Almighty. No one else can even begin to do the job.[36]

Emphasizing the availability of God's mercy until the final moment of death, he continued:

If "Schultz's" conversion was sincere, it means that God gave him a last chance to save his soul, and that "Dutch" took advantage of the offer. It does not mean that God, or His Church, condoned the evil life of "Schultz" but that … God judged he should be given another opportunity to save his soul….

> "Here was the Catholic Church … beckoning into her fold a man who through his entire life had represented everything that the Church abhorred and condemned…."

After all, heaven belongs to God. If He wants "Dutch Schultz" to be there, it is difficult to see what we can do about it. Perhaps, instead of worrying about "Schultz," a somewhat more profitable occupation for us would be to do a little more worrying about our own salvation — to make sure we get there ourselves. We may not be given the opportunity for a death-bed repentance. Relatively few are given that chance.

And whether we meet "Schultz" in heaven or not, there is one individual we are certain to encounter there: a gentleman who was in more or less the same line as "Schultz" — the Thief who, as he was dying on Calvary, asked the Man on the next Cross for forgiveness and who heard that Man say: "This day thou shalt be with Me in Paradise."[37]

Perhaps, on second thought, some of Schultz's last words weren't so nonsensical after all. Is it possible that even Dutch Schultz was given, at the last possible moment, a tiny glimpse of the Blessed Mother Mary's intercession and maternal care when he said, "Mother is the best bet"?

Notes

31. Sann, Paul. *Kill the Dutchman!* 1970. http://killthedutchman.net/.

32. Ibid.

33. Ibid.

34. Ibid.

35. Ibid.

36. Toomey, Fr. John A. "'Schultz' at the Gate." December 1935. http://www.unz.org/Pub/LiteraryDigest-1935nov30-00016a02.

37. Ibid.

CHAPTER 6

Alexis Carrel

June 28, 1873 – November 5, 1944

"Beneath the deep, harsh warnings of my intellectual pride, a smothered dream persists."[38]

— Alexis Carrell

For a very long time, Alexis Carrel — Nobel Prize-winning doctor, inventor (with Charles Lindberg) of the perfusion pump, and organ-transplant pioneer — accepted only the things of science as worthy of trust. He witnessed not one but two miracles at the famous healing shrine at Lourdes, yet persisted in his skepticism for decades after seeing these inexplicable events.

The first of these miracles took place in 1902. The young French doctor went to Lourdes at the request of a colleague who had to bow out of his place on the "white train" at the last minute. These trains were so called because of the color of the ticket — white trains transported the most severely ill patients, attended by doctors and nurses. Carrel, who had abandoned the Catholic faith of his childhood, neither believed in nor expected to see miracles, but he had theories about the power of suggestion and wanted to study the fast rates of healing at the shrine.

He ended up on the same train as Marie Bailly, a young woman with tuberculous peritonitis. In the early twentieth century, the prognosis for this condition was grim, and for Marie, it was as grim as it could possibly be. Her father, mother, and brother had all died of tuberculosis. Marie Bailly was now dying; in fact, her condition was so serious that her doctors had refused to operate. There was nothing more to be done, they said; surgery could kill her.

Given her grave condition, she would not even have been granted a place on a train, but a nurse (who believed as strongly as Marie did in the healing power of Lourdes) managed to sneak Marie onto the train at the last minute. It was there that she met Carrel, and it was a meeting they would both remember for the rest of their lives, although it would be over forty years before he came to terms with the issue of faith.

Marvelous — or Miraculous?

This is what happened at Lourdes in 1902.

The tuberculous peritonitis had caused immense swelling in Marie's abdomen. The doctors, including Carrel, also detected large, hard lumps. Though Marie was near death, she remained convinced that she would be cured. Ironically, Marie's unshakeable faith may have cemented Carrel's refusal to believe in the miraculous nature of what he saw. Since he believed that the power of suggestion might be at play in Lourdes healings, Marie's conviction seemingly supported his theory. What Carrel did not know is that Marie not only believed that she would be cured, she said that the Blessed Mother had communicated to her a reason outside herself for her cure: it was to be for the salvation of another soul.

When it was time for Marie to be taken to the healing water of the pool, she was too weak to be moved. She recalled that instead of immersion, three pitchers of Lourdes water were poured over her belly. The first dousing caused a great deal of pain in her stomach, the second a little less, and the third actually felt pleasant, according to Marie. Within a half hour, her pulse calmed, her abdomen flattened, and the hard lumps were gone. That night she was able to sit up, speak, and have a bite to eat.

The next day, Marie Bailly, who for five months had not taken food without vomiting, got dressed, had a meal, and took a train home on her own. When she arrived home, her family did not recognize her. They demanded proof that she was the same woman who had been near death just a few days before.

Carrel and other doctors followed up closely, speculating on and perhaps clinging to their theories of the power of suggestion. Carrel requested psychiatric tests, which were done every two weeks for four months. Bailly passed every one. She was tested for traces of tuberculosis regularly, and never showed the slightest relapse. She joined the Sisters of Charity but only after they, too, carefully scrutinized her condition, both physical and mental, and were satisfied that she was sane, balanced, and physically healthy. She remained active with the Sisters of Charity until 1937, when she died at the age of fifty-eight.

Carrel was in a precarious position. As a staunch man of science, he hoped that his peers would not learn he had been to Lourdes. Even the rumor of such a thing could affect his career as an assistant anatomy professor at the University of Lyons. However, a local newspaper published a story revealing that he had been present at Marie Bailly's cure. The reporter hinted that Carrel remained a skeptic.

Carrel's surprising response placed him firmly and stubbornly outside all camps. He criticized the religious faithful for what he saw as their gullibility and hasty, premature conclusions. At the same time, he criticized members of the medical community for refusing to face facts that did not line up neatly with prior experience. He knew that something had happened to Marie Bailly, but he was not yet ready to come down on either side of the debate over what that something was. Soon after this, he was forced to leave the university. Ironically, the very center of intellectual inquiry — a university — forced him out for his openness to examining every facet of an issue.

Within months of his encounter with Marie and her healing, Carrel wrote *Journey to Lourdes*, a detailed account of the experience (it wasn't published, however, until five years after his death). In his introduction to Carrel's book, Fr. Stanley Jaki notes that Carrel persisted in calling the cure "marvelous" rather than "miraculous." He was willing to admit that science did not seem able to answer everything, but he was unwilling to make a radical leap of faith and leave his long-nurtured skepticism behind.

In 1910, Carrel witnessed a second miracle at Lourdes. An eighteen-month-old child who had been born blind regained his sight. Still, Alexis Carrel held onto his doubt. Part of the job of science is to explain the natural world, and by training and experience Carrel was well suited for the task. But knowing where observable nature ends and invisible, supernatural events begin can be a tricky business, and it is poignant to read, in *Voyage to Lourdes*, Carrel's description of himself and his faith life. He describes "Lerrac" (Carrel backwards, the pseudonym he gave himself in the account) as one whose religious ideas had been "ground down by the analytic process." He concludes that all that is left to him is "a lovely memory of a delicate and beautiful dream."[39] The book ends with his beautiful, sad and pleading prayer to the Blessed Virgin for faith: "Beneath the deep, harsh warnings of my intellectual pride a smothered dream persists. Alas, it is still only a dream, but the most enchanting of them all. It is the dream of believing in Thee and of loving Thee with the shining spirit of the men of God."[40]

> He concludes that all that is left to him is "a lovely memory of a delicate and beautiful dream."

What Matters at the End

Against this backdrop, Carrell's career thrived. He had been a medical student in 1894 when French president Sadi Carnot was assassinated. Carrel was struck by the fact that the president might have survived if a severed vein could have been repaired. This prompted him to search for new methods of suturing blood vessels and he spent the next nine years developing the technique, experimenting on animals until he perfected it. His work in vascular surgery led to his Nobel Prize in 1912.

Over the years, Carrel's career took him from Lyons to Paris, to Canada, and then to the United States, where he eventually worked at Hull Laboratory with Dr. Charles Guthrie on his vascular suture and transplantation techniques. He then moved on to the Rockefeller Institute where he was able to devote his time entirely to research for the rest of his career, until 1939 when he retired. In 1941, Carrel returned to France, and though he refused a political position as public health director under the Vichy government in occupied France, he did accept directorship of the Foundation for the Study of Human Problems, a German organization. This led to charges of Nazi collaboration when the war was over, an accusation that's debatable. He died before any charges were seriously pursued.

In the last years of his life, a final beacon appeared to this man who had been offered numerous chances to embrace faith. In 1937, Carrel, at the urging of his wife, followed up on a friend's suggestion that he meet Fr. Alexis Presse, a Trappist monk. Carrel was reluctant, but upon meeting the monk immediately felt he was in the presence of a living saint. As they talked, Fr. Presse stressed to Carrel that everything in our lives comes back to love. Paradoxically, this appeal to emotion intrigued the man of science who struggled with purely intellectual explanations of faith.

Fr. Presse and Carrel developed a surprising rapport and became friends. By 1942, Carrel recorded in his diary that he finally believed in God, in an immortal soul, and in the beauty of the Catholic Church's teachings. The grace of his infant baptism had come to full fruition.

In 1944, Alexis Carrel had a heart attack. Informed that Carrel was dying, Fr. Presse jumped on a train and hurried to see him; by the time he arrived, Carrel had already received the last sacraments. "When one approaches one's own death," Carrell said just a few days before he died, "one grasps the nothingness of all things. I have gained fame. The world speaks of me and of my works, yet I am a mere child before God, and a poor child at that."[41]

Alexis Carrel died on November 5, 1944, secure in the knowledge that God is the author of all: faith and reason, science and belief, intellect and emotion, and, perhaps most of all, the miracle of conversion.

Notes

38. Carrel, Alexis. *The Voyage to Lourdes.* Sterling Heights, MI: Real-View-Books, 2007, 94.
39. Ibid., 56.
40. Ibid., 94.
41. Ibid., 35.

Chapter 7

Wallace Stevens

October 2, 1879 – August 2, 1955

I fled Him, down the nights and down the days;
I fled Him, down the arches of the years;
I fled Him, down the labyrinthine ways
Of my own mind; and in the mist of tears
I hid from Him, and under running laughter.[42]

— "The Hound of Heaven"

The insurance executive who never learned to drive set out on foot every morning from his home in Hartford, Connecticut, to his office at the Hartford Accident and Indemnity Company. It was a predictable, rhythmic walk. The steady, contemplative pace of the two-and-a-half-mile sojourn lent itself to the chief undertaking of the man in the grey suit: the composition of poetry. Once at his office, he plucked scraps of scribbled dreams, fragments of longing, and strips of imagination from his pockets, and asked his secretary to type them up in clean, orderly lines. No one who knew the poetry-writing vice president would suspect that while on vacation in Key West, Florida, he would punch Ernest Hemingway in the face.

The stories vary, as is often the case when egos and alcohol are involved. Both Stevens and Hemingway agreed that the fight began at a cocktail party. Stevens implied that strong but drunken disagreements on relatively benign subjects led to fisticuffs. Hemingway told the story with more pizazz. His sister Ursula was supposedly reduced to tears when she heard Wallace Stevens bad-mouthing her brother at the party. When she fled to find Hemingway, Stevens allegedly remarked that he wished he had Hemingway in front of him at that moment so that he could "knock him out with a single punch."[43]

When Hemingway found Stevens, Stevens took that swing, only to have Hemingway retaliate and knock him to the ground. Several times. When Stevens' fist finally connected with Hemingway's face, he broke his hand on his opponent's jaw. Stevens lied to his wife and daughter (who were at home in sedate Hartford), saying that his black eye and broken hand happened when he fell down a flight of stairs. Hemingway later wrote of the two hundred twenty-five-pound, six-foot-three poet:

> Anyway, last night Mr. Stevens comes over to make up and we are made up. But on mature reflection I don't know anybody needed to be hit worse than Mr. S. Was very pleased last night to see how large Mr. Stevens was and am sure that if I had had a good look at him before it all started would not have felt up to hitting him. But can assure you that there is no one like Mr. Stevens to go down in a spectacular fashion especially into a large puddle of water in the street … where all took place.…[44]

The Grey-Flannel Poet

Wallace Stevens was an American Modernist poet, a Pulitzer Prize winner, a lawyer, an insurance executive, and he was always an enigma to me. When I first encountered his poetry, I found it to be dense, cold, and distant, lush in imagery, but seemingly without heart or soul. He was obviously intellectual, sometimes amusing, nearly always removed, but fascinating in his many layers. His poetry is cerebral and often incomprehensible, but can also be emotionally arresting. Robert Frost, with whom Stevens had several disagreements (though no fistfights) didn't care for Stevens' work "because it purports to make me think," Frost said.[45]

In an online conversation with another writer a few years ago, I contrasted Wallace Stevens' style with that of the infinitely more accessible American poet, Billy Collins, who is known for his readability:

> Billy Collins is like the pal you love and go out with for coffee … the friend with whom you never have a conflict, because you always know exactly what he means. And he gets you, too, and you love him for that. And then you order more coffee and sigh and think, "If only everything could be this easy."

Wallace Stevens is like your inscrutable uncle who isn't always kind, and sometimes doesn't seem to want you around, but who's so complex and interesting that you keep having him over. And when you pin him down on something, and whisper to your mother, who's sitting next to you, that now you know why he's like this, he smiles cryptically, and looks away.

Your coffee friend would, of course, be insulted at being analyzed, but your uncle practically begs for it.

Stevens' poetry does beg analysis, and even his biggest fans and some scholars confess that after probing dissection they don't always understand him. Influenced by the Romantic poets, Wallace Stevens spent the bulk of his literary life exploring the nature of reality and the reality of the imagination. As a young man, Stevens once wrote in his journal that he would make many sacrifices to be a St. Augustine, but his attraction to Augustine waned, and he soon thereafter rejected Christianity. Much of his poetry celebrated a pagan view of the world and explored the life of the mind. So he was stranded with a quandary: what are we to do with the innate desire and will to believe when we no longer believe in God? Stevens spent his life seeking the answer to that question. He looked for certitude in the universe while lamenting the lack of certainty in anything.

Wallace Stevens was a contradiction: the passionate poet who spent his days in a business suit. On the other hand, perhaps his life exemplifies not a contradiction, but the human condition — the need we all have to reconcile ourselves to the world in which we live. Wallace Stevens was simply another questioning pilgrim on a long walk toward the truth.

The Muse Resists

Born in Reading, Pennsylvania, Wallace Stevens (he had no middle name) was raised by well-to-do parents with a Calvinist background and a strong Puritan work ethic. It was a religious tradition that Stevens would reject by the time he was a young man, and whose rejection he would struggle with for years to come.

Wallace had a normal, uneventful childhood, though he did display early gifts for writing and scholarship. His father encouraged his literary pursuits, and Stevens ended up at Harvard, where he won every writing award the university offered. He penned poetry, literary sketches, stories, and acted as editor of two Harvard papers. When Stevens could no longer afford to continue at Harvard, he dropped out and went to work as a journalist in New York City. He found the work tedious, and looked forward to evenings with music, theater, and his own writing.

Stagnating, Stevens approached his father about how he could fully devote himself to the literary life. His father, however, was a practical man and informed his son he'd better get himself to law school, which Stevens did at the age of twenty-two. He didn't abandon his literary dreams, but they were put on hold as he concentrated on studies and the launch of a career. He graduated from law school, passed the bar exam in 1904, and worked as a lawyer until 1908, when he went to work for an insurance firm in their legal department. He was enormously successful, eventually becoming the vice-president of the Hartford Company and he stayed with the industry for the rest of his life.

On a summer night in 1904, Wallace met a honey-haired, blue-eyed, eighteen-year-old girl who possessed a classic beauty (she was later the model for the Mercury Winged Liberty dime). Stevens was smitten with the girl. He found in Elsie a wispy muse, a treasure. She embodied the exquisite air he sought to capture in his writing, and his "faery," as he called her, renewed his creative spirit.

He wrote poetry to, for, and about her. He wanted to marry her, but promised himself he would not do so until he was absolutely sure he was financially stable. The enigma who believed in a world with no objective certainty courted his wife-to-be for five years, until he felt objectively certain that he could support a spouse.

In 1909, Stevens and Elsie were wed, much to the chagrin of Stevens' family, who strongly disapproved of the match. They found in Elsie an average, common girl, nowhere near the intellectual equal of Wallace. Wallace's sister described Elsie as "a pretty doll-like creature who never said anything."[46] Stevens' father objected loudly to the union, and father and son had an ugly fight that ended with a threat from Wallace: if the family could not or would not accept Elsie, he would never return to their home. He made good on his threat. He married his muse, his family did not attend the wedding, and he did not see his father again before his father's death two years later.

> Just a couple of years before his marriage, Stevens had thrown his Bible in the trash in order to make a bold statement about where he stood on religion.

Initially, the marriage seemed happy, but an interesting and difficult dynamic began to develop. Modernism, which the young Stevens embraced in his work, was a rejection of all things traditional. For Stevens, it was the perfect imaginative construct — it invited the poet to become the creator of all things. Just a couple of years before his marriage, Stevens had thrown his Bible in the trash in order to make a bold statement about where he stood on religion — modernism was his new belief system.

But it was not only through his poetry that Wallace sought to create reality anew. He saw Elsie as a blank slate, and carried the conceit that she would be made in his image. She did her best to comply. He asked her to wear particular kinds of clothing, even specific outfits, as if he were ordering a meal to be served just as he liked it. He recommended lofty books and reading that would shape her mind and mold her into the wife he wanted her to be. Stevens attempted to construct both marriage and the nature of reality into ideals based on the power of the imagination. Perhaps neither one could stand the strain.

With business thriving and writing a constant, Stevens saw his poetry published in several influential magazines; he gained a reputation as a fine writer who could tackle wry, satirical humor as well as navigate grave, existential waters. In 1923, when Stevens was forty-three years old, his first volume of poetry, *Harmonium*, was published. The following year his only child Holly was born. Just as he had postponed marriage until he felt financially secure, Stevens had put off having children until he was certain he could provide for a family. It should have been the prime of life — ambitions realized, a growing family, and financial security. But as Stevens' poetry became more successful, Elsie grew unhappy and spiteful. She felt abandoned by Wallace's devotion to his books and writing, and nursed a strong sense of betrayal that he had given to the world, by way of publication, poems she'd thought of as private correspondence.

This "betrayal" so infuriated her that she would not even allow a single room in their house to be used as a library. Stevens kept most of his books boxed up in his attic. The more obsessed Stevens became with his books — collecting unread special editions, refusing to purchase used copies of books — the more Elsie hated them. The more Stevens displayed, through his poetry in particular, his rejection of religion, the more Elsie embraced her puritanical upbringing. She banned alcohol, looked down on smoking, criticized the slightest dietary overindulgence.

They entered an unspoken combat zone, each choosing a side and defending with chilled silences. Stevens often sent Elsie home to Reading for long visits. He was happier when she was away. He could walk for hours, write, read, and feel he was himself again. He traveled to Key West, and hid from his wife how much alcohol he consumed on his trips south.

Elsie could never be the woman Stevens had conjured in his imagination, and he was sometimes embarrassed by her, worried about what she would say at dinner parties. He befriended writers, publishers, artists, and the avant-garde, reveling in such company, but Elsie, despising all that she was not, and feeling unappreciated for all that she was, sniffed to friends that she found her husband's poetry to be affected.

Though his marriage was bleak, Wallace loved his daughter very much and the two of them were close. Perhaps Stevens found consolations in art and fatherhood that he was unable to attain in marriage. In some of his most touching poems, such as "The Snowman" and "Thirteen Ways of Looking at a Blackbird," we sense something deeply longed for that is just out of reach, and always will be.

Silent Shadows

After Holly's birth in 1924, Stevens had stopped writing for several years, citing fatherhood and general busyness, but when he started publishing again, recognition of his work grew. By the early 1950s he gained a reputation as one of the premiere poets of the twentieth century. In 1955 came *The Collected Poems of Wallace Stevens* and with it, the Pulitzer Prize, as well as his second National Book Award.

That year brought something else into Stevens' life. He initially thought he was having minor digestive problems. He chalked the pain up to recent inactivity and the inability to get out walking as often as he would have liked. Though convinced it was nothing serious, he let himself be hospitalized. The doctors told his family that he had stomach cancer, but Holly chose to keep the terminal diagnosis from her father in an attempt to keep his spirits up.

Fr. Arthur Hanley, chaplain at St. Francis hospital, visited Stevens when he was first hospitalized. They talked frequently on subjects from books to the faith. Fr. Hanley amused Stevens with his Middle English rendition of a short passage from *The Canterbury*

Tales. Stevens told the kindly priest his stories about visiting St. Patrick's Cathedral over the years.

For a man who gave up on organized religion, St. Patrick's Cathedral in New York had held a curious lifelong allure for Stevens. He had sometimes slipped into the church as a young man just to spend a few minutes. In the final year of his life, he periodically passed through its ornate front doors and meditated in the quiet of the cathedral's gothic interior, which is, like Stevens' poetry, lush, dense, and dripping with sacred imagery. In the quiet within, St. Patrick's Cathedral holds the secret found in every tabernacle in the world: behind a small, locked door is Jesus in the Blessed Sacrament. The poet's silent visits to this sacred space perhaps drew him closer, without his explicit assent, to the living Christ.

During Stevens' first hospitalization in April of 1955, Fr. Hanley sensed that the poet felt emptiness, but he also believed Stevens had accepted general belief in a deity. In fact, in 1951, Stevens had written to Sister Bernetta Quinn, an occasional correspondent, and stated that he was not an atheist, though he no longer believed in the god of his boyhood. Despite his rejection of organized religion, Stevens could not ultimately give up the will to believe. Still, he was troubled by the doctrine of hell, and he and Fr. Hanley discussed free will, mercy, and justice. They talked of grace and of the freedom to reject it. Stevens shared with Fr. Hanley that he had exchanged correspondence with Sister Madaleva, a poet and the president of St. Mary's College, on similar topics. (This correspondence did not survive.)

Finally, when Stevens was admitted to the hospital again in July of 1955, he asked Fr. Hanley to baptize him. Fr. Hanley discreetly complied, and later wrote that the baptism seemed to bring Stevens great peace. According to Fr. Hanley, Stevens said, "Now I'm in the fold."[47]

A friend, Margaret Powers, said that in his last days he had a crucifix and a St. Christopher medal from Margaret's daughter, Julie, beside him, on his pillow.

Fr. Hanley and his bishop thought it wise to keep the conversion quiet; the news would upset Elsie and others. Stevens' daughter, Holly, never believed or accepted that her father had converted. She speculated that the priest was merely being a pest in his final days, and when news of the conversion became known in the late 1970s, Holly vehemently denied that it had happened. Perhaps we'll never know all the facts, but we do know that, no matter how close we are, what transpires in the heart of a loved one can be indecipherable.

In "Sunday Morning," a poem that Stevens said was about paganism, the poet questioned divinity, wondering what it is, what it's worth if it comes to us only in dreams or in shadows that are still and quiet. Wallace Stevens spent his entire life sifting through shadows and dreams in a strenuous effort to define and create reality. In the end, he came to believe that divinity can venture out of those "silent shadows" and come to us incarnate, come to us as something — as Someone — more real than anything else we can imagine.

Wallace Stevens died on August 2, 1955, at the age of seventy-five. His last words, spoken peacefully to his daughter and his grandson, were, "Good night."[48]

Notes

42. Thompson, Francis. *The Hound of Heaven.* N.p.: Project Gutenberg, 2009. http://www.gutenberg.org/files/30730/30730-h/30730-h.htm.

43. Baker, Carlos, ed. *Ernest Hemingway, Selected Letters, 1917–1961.* New York: Charles Scribner's Sons, 1981, 439.

44. Ibid.

45. Haskell, Arlo. "The Trouble with Robert Frost and Wallace Stevens." Littoral. http://www.kwls.org/littoral/post_11/.

46. Brazeau, Peter, ed. *Parts of a World, Wallace Stevens Remembered, An Oral Biography.* San Francisco: North Point Press, 1985, 260.

47. Ibid., 295.

48. Richardson, Joan. *Wallace Stevens The Later Years, 1923–1955.* New York: Beech Tree Books William Morrow, 1988, 427.

Chapter 8

John Wayne

May 26, 1907 – June 11, 1979

"There is nothing free except the grace of God. You cannot earn that or deserve it."[49]
— From *True Grit*

He was a big guy to be a stowaway. Hidden on the SS *Malolo*, a steamship headed from San Francisco to Honolulu, the twenty-year-old college student did his best to blend with other passengers, to pass as a paying customer while bunking down at night in an empty cabin he'd located. But meals presented a challenge, and four days into the trip, his hollow belly forced him to confess his folly to the captain. Marion Morrison was promptly locked up for the rest of the cruise, until the ship returned to San Francisco a month later. Upon docking, the captain turned him over to the police who cuffed and jailed him. Luckily, the police chief was the father of one of Morrison's friends. He convinced the SS *Malolo's* owners not to press charges against the student, who had foolishly stowed away on a lark after failing to find work in San Francisco, and sent him back to Los Angeles on a train. Marion Morrison was more than a little depressed.

True Grit

Everyone called him "Duke." He'd gotten the moniker at age eleven from the firemen whose station he passed every day with his enormous pet, an Airedale named Duke. The firemen always said hello to the boy and his dog, and started calling Morrison "Little Duke." He preferred that to Marion, a name he was teased about and despised, and he preferred it to Morrison, which he'd been encouraging pals to call him. Duke fit, and it stuck, at the boy's insistence.

Now Duke was depressed. He'd spent the previous two years at the University of Southern California, majoring in pre-law. His father's job-hopping and drinking had meant his family never had a lot of money, so he was grateful for the football scholarship — it paid tuition and provided one meal per weekday. To further feed and support himself, the Iowa-born student took a part-time job in the frat house where he'd just pledged. He waited on and bused tables for his Sigma Chi brothers. Despite their respect for Duke's brains and brawn, the menial work left him with a gnawing feeling of inferiority, the same thing many of the other "scholarship boys" felt.

Playing football had made up for a lot, but that was going south. The summer after his freshman year, Duke and some friends were bodysurfing. Duke reveled in time at the ocean and he and his friends bodysurfed as often as they could. But this time, his eyes on the girls instead of on his timing, Duke caught a wave late and was thrown. He wound up with a separated shoulder and possibly a broken collarbone. When football practice started, Morrison was hurting. He tried his best for as long as he could, working through the agonizing pain and attempting to get through the season with a shoulder harness, but his football career, and the financial aid that went with it, was over. By the end of his sophomore year, Duke was in debt, discouraged, and considering dropping out. That was when he headed to San Francisco, failed to find a summer job, and snuck aboard the SS *Malolo*. Now he was back, and prospects looked no better.

He wondered if he could get a part-time job with the film director John Ford as he had once before. In his freshman year, Duke and a number of other USC football players had been tapped as extras for movies, and Ford had spotted Duke on a set. He asked if he was one of the Trojans. When Duke said yes, Ford asked him to drop into position. Duke obliged, and Ford kicked his hands out from under him, laughing. "And you call yourself a football player. I'll bet you couldn't even take me out."[50] Within seconds, that's exactly what the Duke did. He charged at the director with the full force of his six-foot-three-inch frame, smashing Ford to the ground. Everyone on the set froze, waiting for the Hollywood director, who was notorious for his temper, to hand the young punk his head. Instead, Ford exploded with laughter. He loved Duke's true grit. The two men would end up lifelong friends.

But right now, Duke was a scared, confused kid. He approached Ford again, and began earning a little money doing prop work for him over the summer. As his junior year approached, Morrison faced some facts. With a bad shoulder, no scholarship, and the realization that he would never feel comfortable in the big-money world of his fellow pre-law frat brothers, Duke turned to Ford for career advice. He asked about long-term prospects in Hollywood. The "mixture of Irish and Jewish accents, old money and new, hustle, greed, and optimism" made him feel at home.[51] In Hollywood, he wouldn't have to worry about his lack of pedigree. Ford assured him he could help him find a way to make a living.

We know what happened next. He adopted the stage name John Wayne, and this American icon of masculinity and patriotism eventually appeared in more than 175 movies. He won an Academy Award for his portrayal of crusty Rooster Cogburn in *True Grit*. He played dozens of cowboys in a wealth of Westerns, and was Maureen O'Hara's *Quiet Man*. If you remember an old war movie, it probably starred the Duke. His big break had come at the age of thirty-two when, after appearing in a number of B movies, he struck gold with his role in John Ford's *Stagecoach*. From then on, there was nothing little about Little Duke.

Much-Married Megastar

On the personal front, things were often rockier for the star. He met Josephine Saenz, his first of three wives, while in college. They dated for seven years as Wayne tried to curry favor with Josephine's father, a wealthy, prominent businessman. Mr. Saenz was unimpressed with the prospect of a part-time actor for a son-in-law, especially one who refused to convert to the family's Catholic faith. But as Wayne's career took off, resistance to the marriage softened and in 1933, Marion Morrison and Josephine Saenz were wed. They had four children who were raised as Catholics by their mother, but the marriage ended after only twelve years. Josie's world revolved around her faith, her family, and Los Angeles society. Duke, on the other hand, loved the stuff of Hollywood: long working hours on location, and drinking with his movie buddies. Staid dinners with priests or society's elite were not his idea of amusement.

In 1941, Duke met Esperanza "Chata" Bauer, a woman with a murky past and an electric presence. They began an affair, and by 1945 Wayne left Josie and his children, then aged ten, eight, five, and four, for Chata. Josie accepted the divorce only as a legal, civil path to secure a financial future for her children. While John Wayne was alive, she never remarried.

Duke and Chata were in love, but they were a volatile mix. Both liked to drink, which led to misunderstandings and storms. One night, Wayne stumbled home after an all-night wrap party to find himself locked out of his house. He broke a glass panel to reach inside and unlock the door, then stumbled in and passed out on the couch. Chata came at him with a loaded pistol. Depending on whose story one believes, she either thought he was an intruder or suspected him of an affair with actress Gail Russell. The stuff of melodrama was typical of the tumultuous pair.

In 1952, while still married to Chata, he met a young actress named Pilar Pallette on a movie set in Peru. Both were smitten, and they married in 1954 when Wayne's divorce from Bauer was finalized and Pilar's first marriage annulled. But it was a messy beginning — their secret affair, a pregnancy, and an abortion. When Pilar told Wayne she was pregnant, he assured her he'd be there for her if she wanted to have the baby. But she worried for his career. Raised a Catholic, Pilar later admitted feeling horrible guilt over her decision; she and Wayne went on to have three children. At their wedding, Pilar requested that the word "obey" be struck from their vows. Duke conceded. "None of the others ever obeyed me anyway," he said.[52]

How did this thrice-married, hard-drinking, larger-than-life megastar make his leap to Catholicism? Faith danced around John Wayne all of his adult life. All three of his wives had been raised Catholic, and all seven of his children were brought up in the Church. His first wife, Josie, who prayed for Duke's conversion till the end, convinced him to attend numerous parish events with her. He sometimes complained to friends that he was up to his neck in Catholics, but perhaps as he interacted with genuine, faithful people, misconceptions and prejudices fell away. Did the classic church potluck plant seeds of conversion?

How Does All This Stuff Work?

Despite his early upbringing in the Presbyterian Church, Duke never had any denominational loyalty and was impatient with the infighting of Christianity. Wayne's son Michael thought his father was a man who quietly believed in God even as he shunned church attendance. "There must be a higher power," Wayne said in the year he died, "or how does all this stuff work?"[53]

Though he didn't embrace Catholicism, it permeated his life. He was convinced that his children's faithfulness, and their Catholic education, as well as the devotion of their Catholic mothers to their families, had made them great people. (One of his sons, Patrick, even considered the priesthood for a time.) Perhaps Wayne's multiple-marriage situation proved an impediment in terms of the Catholic faith. (In addition to two divorces, he and Pilar separated in 1973, though they never divorced. He then began a relationship with his secretary, Pat Stacy.) Or perhaps conversion just never looked like a realistic, practical possibility.

Catholic priest Fr. Matthew Muñoz, who knew Wayne simply as "Granddaddy," hints that obstacles to his grandfather's conversion toppled slowly as Wayne grew in knowledge of Catholicism. "After a while," Fr. Muñoz said, "he kind of got a sense that the common secular vision of what Catholics are and what his own experience actually was were becoming two greatly different things."[54]

In the mid-1960s, Duke was fighting a persistent cough. His wife urged him to have it checked, and since he needed to renew an insurance policy anyway, he had a physical. When he returned to the clinic the next day for results, he was subjected to an extensive round of X-rays. As he waited, he ran into the technician who'd performed the tests. The young tech revealed what he thought the star already knew: it was lung cancer. Duke was stunned, and the technician was mortified. He panicked and repeatedly apologized for letting slip news that should have come from the doctor. Then he worried, loudly and fearfully, about getting fired for his indiscretion. In spite of his shock about the cancer, Wayne kindly reassured the frightened young man that it was okay. "Don't worry, kid," he said. "I won't tell anybody."[55] When the doctor delivered the cancer diagnosis two hours later, the actor pretended he was hearing the news for the first time.

John Wayne, whom the whole world saw as invincible, beat the lung cancer, as everyone knew he would. He became a vocal advocate for those fighting the disease, and his family eventually established the John Wayne Cancer Institute.

Then in 1974, when the star began battling repeated respiratory illnesses, he feared that the lung cancer had returned, but the doctors told him not to worry. Symptoms of seemingly unrelated illnesses plagued him over the next few years until finally, in 1978, an accurate diagnosis was made. John Wayne had stomach cancer. He deteriorated quickly. By the following year, he was extremely sick, wasting away, and often hospitalized.

Wayne had watched his friend John Ford suffer from the same kind of cancer just a few years before. Ford had been a Catholic; he died with priests in the room and a rosary in his hand. Ford's faith and its uplifting effect on his life and death were etched into Wayne's psyche. Duke remembered the comfort and courage Catholicism had given his friend.

On May 14, 1979, Michael asked his father if it would be okay to have Archbishop Marcos McGrath come and visit. Duke said yes, and the two men spent an afternoon together talking. Wayne agreed that day to call for a priest before he died. Duke had often joked with his family that he was a "cardiac Catholic," that at the last minute he'd call in a priest. Now he made that promise.

With the end near, Wayne was in constant agony. The nation that had always loved this icon of America rallied, eager to acknowledge the Duke's contribution to the country. A special gold medal was proposed. Actress Maureen O'Hara testified to a House subcommittee, suggesting that the medal be called, "John Wayne, American." President Jimmy Carter approved, and a letter was sent to the hospitalized hero.

Two days before he died, Wayne, in tremendous pain, agreed when his son Patrick asked him if they should call the priest now. "Yeah," Duke said, "I think that's a good idea."[56] Fr. Robert Curtis, UCLA Medical Center chaplain, arrived. He baptized the dying man, probably conditionally, as Wayne had grown up in a Christian church, and administered last rites. That night, Wayne fell into a coma. "I don't know the technicalities of the Church or what constitutes a conversion," said Michael. "But Dad did die in the Church."[57]

> Duke had often joked with his family that he was a "cardiac Catholic," that at the last minute he'd call in a priest.

The man who had achieved worldwide fame was buried quietly in an unmarked grave, the location known only to a few select intimates for many years. His final resting place, now acknowledged as Pacific View Memorial Cemetery, overlooks the Pacific Ocean, the place he loved, and the place that had changed the direction of his life by way of a simple surfing accident.

Notes

49. Portis, Charles. *True Grit*. New York: The Overlook Press, 2010, 40.

50. Roberts, Randy, and James S. Olson. *John Wayne, American.* New York: The Free Press, 1995, 61.

51. Ibid., 65.

52. Ibid., 415.

53. Ibid., 639.

54. Kerr, David. "My Grandaddy, John Wayne, actor and Catholic convert." Catholic News Agency. http://www.catholicnewsagency.com/news/my-granddaddy-john-wayne-actor-and-catholic-convert/.

55. Roberts, Randy, and James S. Olson. *John Wayne, American.* New York: The Free Press, 1995, 508.

56. Ibid., 639.

57. Ibid., 644.

CHAPTER 9

Kenneth Clark

July 13, 1903 – May 21, 1983

> "Beauty is truth, truth beauty," — that is all
> Ye know on earth, and all ye need to know.
> — John Keats, *Ode on a Grecian Urn*

Fr. Robert Barron, creator of the sweeping documentary series, *Catholicism*, said, "When, a few years ago, I embarked on the production of a ten-part documentary about Catholicism, emphasizing both the truth and the artistic beauty of the church, Kenneth Clark was my model and inspiration."[58]

In 1966, Fr. Barron's artistic and intellectual role model lunched with David Attenborough, head of the British Broadcasting Corporation. The art historian and the media executive discussed the possibility of a BBC TV series, though at the time neither could have suspected that the resulting program — *Civilisation* — would become "the most successful television series of its kind ever made," as the *New York Times* later said.[59] A masterful series documenting Western art, philosophy, and architecture through the ages, it became Kenneth Clark's magnum opus, a culmination of the myriad talents of this critic, historian, writer, lecturer, and deep lover of the arts who had a desire to bring beauty to the masses.

The response to Clark's *Civilisation* was staggering. Groundbreaking in format, sweeping in scope, and beautiful to behold, viewers responded with passion. They wanted to see, hear, and even touch the genius who had created and narrated the series. People wrote letters saying he'd given them a reason to live, that his work had literally stopped them from committing suicide. Clark was overwhelmed; he couldn't shake the feeling that he was a fraud.

When he was presented a medal at the National Gallery of Art in Washington, D.C., the energy and reaction of the crowd was overpowering. Clark held back tears as he made his way up the aisle to accept the award. He suppressed them as long as he could, but halfway to the podium, a torrent burst forth. The man who grew up feeling unloved by his own mother had become the darling of the world.

A Jumble of Neuroses

The child who would become Sir Kenneth Mackenzie Clark was born in London in 1903 to Kenneth and Alice Clark. Kenneth's father was a wealthy, seemingly happy man who happened to have a problem with alcohol. Kenneth, always called K by family and friends, took care of his father when the senior Clark got staggering drunk. K's mother was a painfully reserved and distant woman. She refused to listen to music or attend church for fear that such things would rouse emotion, and she eschewed Christmas celebrations for the same reason. As an adult, Kenneth could not recall ever being touched by his mother. It was not a happy childhood, though Clark could not admit that to himself. He assumed, as children of alcoholics often do, that his home life was the norm. A lonely child, K engaged in pastimes unusual for one so young, such as regularly rearranging his parents' many paintings.

Art appreciation came naturally to the boy. K's father adored art and presented his seven-year-old son with a book about the Louvre. It became a well-read companion and sixty-three years later K could still rhapsodize about the paintings that sprang to life from its pages. (Coincidentally, he also nursed an extended adolescent fascination with the art of Aubrey Beardsley, a later subject of this book.)

The shame of a parent's alcoholism, the accompanying secret-keeping, and the constant emotional distancing taught young Kenneth not to trust in people or in feelings. But, he discovered, art allowed feelings to grow and flourish, even if those feelings were for an object. Objects never disappointed. Kenneth Clark once even said he was able to "enjoy storms at sea because he was too unfeeling to find them terrifying."[60]

Clark was a jumble of neuroses — a highly intelligent man with very little confidence. A promising lecturer and writer by the time he was eighteen years old, he was also a hypochondriac who was convinced as a teen that he would die of a paralytic disease before he was thirty. Such fear and insecurity would linger for years, and his desire for love was clouded by a fear of commitment.

While studying art history at Trinity College, Oxford, Kenneth easily established himself as a standout. While other students tacked hunting posters on their dormitory walls, Clark displayed an impressive array of paintings, including Van Goghs and Picassos, which he'd begun collecting as a teenager. "He was cocooned in a civilization of his own up there," a friend said.[61] Fellow students and professors alike noticed him, whispered, made predictions as he passed by about what this brilliant young scholar would one day accomplish.

As final exams at Trinity neared, K wondered what he would do next. At the suggestion of mentor Charlie Bell, director of the Ashmolean museum, he started writing his first book, on the Gothic Revival. Bell offered K his extensive notes on the subject, saying he'd never get around to writing a book on it himself. Clark was initially intimidated — he didn't know what the Gothic Revival was — but he accepted Bell's offer and set to work.

At the same time, Kenneth's friend, Gordon Waterfield, asked K if he would look after his fiancee, Jane Martin, while Gordon was out of town for work. It was an ill-fated request — Kenneth fell in love with Jane, who was everything he felt he was not: warm and outgoing, spontaneous, open, and honest. He wooed her and won. Waterfield, informed by mail, gallantly let Jane go, feigning relief and citing his lack of financial readiness for a family. But he was heartbroken. How could Jane prefer his friend?

She preferred him so strongly that she submerged a great deal of herself to make the relationship work. Jane and Kenneth were married in 1927 in a simple ceremony, contrary to Jane's

wishes. She wanted a traditional wedding with fanfare and flourish, but Kenneth knew his mother, with her hatred of anything
showy or emotional, would hate that. So K, who avoided conflict
at all costs, chose to disappoint his bride rather than stand up to
Alice. He literally stayed away from Jane, traveling with friends in
Europe, for three months. He then hastily set a date and returned
home the day before the wedding. And he got his wish. To say the
wedding was understated is an understatement. Jane did not have a
wedding dress, and there were no bridesmaids. There was no music,
no champagne, no reception, and nearly no one in attendance. If
Alice ever allowed herself to be pleased, the wedding must have
delighted her.

And Jane must have loved K very much to put up with such
passive-aggressive antics. She threw herself into her marriage, learn-
ing about art and culture for her husband's sake. She was an eager
student, sitting at Kenneth's feet, soaking up his extensive knowledge and expertise. Their first son, Alan Kenneth Mackenzie Clark,
was born in 1928, followed four years later by twins, Colin and
Colette. K's book *The Gothic Revival* was published in 1928. Re-
viewers loved it, and at the age of twenty-seven, Kenneth Clark was
established as a budding success in the art world.

Moments of Vision, Years of Dysfunction

His prowess only grew. He became the professional assistant to Bernard Berenson, a highly regarded expert on Italian Renaissance art,
and accepted a job at the Ashmolean Museum, inaugurating his
tenure with an old childhood hobby: he rearranged and rehung all
the pictures. But Clark nurtured a secret ambition. He wanted to
become director of London's National Gallery, one of the top museums in the world, on a par with Paris's Louvre and the Metropoli-
tan Museum of Art in New York City. No one as young as Clark
had ever held the post. He was certain it was a pipe dream, but
through influential connections it happened. On New Year's Day,
1934, Kenneth Clark strode into his new office. The man who'd

feared he would die of paralysis before age thirty realized, at that very age, his greatest ambition.

The shy, malcontent boy had become a successful professional with a list of friends that read like a cultural Who's Who including such artists as Henry Moore, Graham Sutherland, and Myfanwy Piper, and American writer Edith Wharton, composer Benjamin Britten, and Queen Elizabeth. K's first impression of the Queen was amusing: "What a delightful person she was, and how congenial and what a pity about her clothes."[62] Not intimidated by royalty, he was a frequent dinner guest at Windsor Castle and once noted that they prepared "very good grub."[63]

Adding to his list of accomplishments, he was knighted in 1937, an honor that meant little to him.

His accomplishments at the National Gallery, however, were bold, admirable, brave, and worthy of honor. He worked on much-needed particulars such as lighting and the restoration of paintings. During World War II, Clark helped transport priceless paintings to safe havens during the London Blitz. With the National Gallery in disuse after the paintings were moved, he set up daily concerts there. He established the War Artists' Committee, to keep artists working, and took a position as the head of films in the Ministry of Information. He got twenty-five documentaries off the ground and proved to himself and to others that no matter what the medium, he could master it and use it to share beauty with everyone. Nevertheless, in time the weight of managing the Gallery's internal strife and petty staff problems left Clark yearning to abandon administrative work. He left to become a full-time writer, producing, among other works, an extremely successful book about Leonardo da Vinci that is still in print.

The war had perhaps brought out the best in K's professional life, but heralded difficulties in private. Jane and the children had gone to the country to escape the air raids, leaving K on his own. Jane, a trying spouse in the best of times, was moody and had temper tantrums and unpredictable outbursts, which were probably related to her dependence on a cocaine-based medication for sinusitis. Clark dealt with the difficulties by avoiding them, turning his affection to a younger woman, the first of his affairs.

Jane, in turn, dealt with the affair by ignoring it, hoping it would go away. She then changed tactics, and became a kind of dysfunctional participant in the affair. If K's girlfriend got angry about his family time, Jane urged him to give her a call and offer comfort. Just as she had submerged her rights and wishes when they first married, she submerged them now in a desperate effort to hold on to her husband, whatever the cost. When K decided to end the affair, he displayed what many had come to know as classic Clark arrogance: he asked his wife's advice on how to let his mistress down gently.

> Clark perhaps rationalized the moment as "just a feeling," and feelings could not be trusted. He dismissed them.

Jane, depressed and dispirited, would never be the same again. Had she known the reason for the end of the affair, she would have descended even further into the depths of her sadness. Clark had begun a new affair, this one — which lasted for fourteen years — with artist and family friend Mary Kessell.

K was now writing, lecturing, and broadcasting for the BBC, and publishing well-received books, when suddenly one day he felt something he had never felt before: a kind of divine inspiration. He could not explain the feeling or its origin, he knew only that he had felt an insight: spiritual enlightenment and artistic vision were related. Perhaps, he mused, they were the same thing. His famous lecture "Moments of Vision" grew out of the experience, but the momentum faded. Clark perhaps rationalized the moment as "just a feeling," and feelings could not be trusted. He dismissed them.

An Utter Fraud?

A brief stint with the new Independent Television Authority (ITA) excited Clark as he considered how this new medium called TV could bring art to the masses. As projects became realities, however, K realized he had no control over the quality of the programming, and that frustration, combined with the lack of funding, prompted him to leave. Without a nine-to-five job and no new writing inspiration, K floundered. His long commute for the ITA work, and little family time, had further widened the gap between Jane and K. He indulged in another affair, puttered in his garden, walked his dogs, and told his girlfriend he had just two ambitions left in life: to lose a little weight and improve his handwriting.

Then a lifeline appeared. A new television project, *Is Art Necessary?*, wasn't an immediate success, but Clark dug in with renewed enthusiasm. He honed it into something worthwhile and engaging. He began teaching and lecturing again, and eventually his brainchild, *Civilisation*, was born. Every path Kenneth Clark had walked led to this destination. *Civilisation*, the ten-part program and the best-selling book, became a cultural phenomenon.

Clark's new level of celebrity was dizzying. He'd always wanted to share the splendor of art with the masses, but now he found the reaction of the masses incomprehensible. He had aimed to make the series about art and culture. Why had it become about him?

The night he received the medal at the National Gallery of Art in Washington, D.C., he felt "like a doctor called to the scene of a disaster, who was being inundated with desperate pleas for help from those affected. But he was not a doctor, let alone a prophet of hope…. He was an utter fraud."[64]

Bewildered by his wildly conflicting feelings, Clark could only call on whatever god was out there. He wasn't entirely sure why he felt he needed forgiveness, but he asked for it.

One day Clark received a fan letter about *Civilisation* from a man named Edward Rice, with whom K had mutual friends. Clark met with Edward and his wife, Nolwen, and Clark's final relationship with a woman began. Edward had cancer, and had become an invalid, while Jane's substance abuse, compounded by drinking, had worsened. She took tumbles in public, broke bones, had become forgetful. K and Nolwen, who felt like kindred spirits, sympathized with one another as they cared for their failing spouses.

In 1973, Jane had a stroke and contracted an inflammatory disease the treatment of which resulted in mental confusion. She died in November of 1976. Nolwen had lost Edward as well, and she and K were married the following November, 1977.

My True Colors

By the early 1980s, K's health had also deteriorated. In short succession, he dealt with a prostate operation, a heart condition, arteriosclerosis, a bad hip, and the beginning of Parkinson's disease. In mid-May, 1983, K did something that would have surprised old friends and many fans: he called for a priest, made a confession, and was received into the Catholic Church. A week later, following surgery for a broken hip, he was failing. He called on the priest once again, received the Eucharist, lost consciousness, and died that night.

News of the conversion didn't come out until a memorial service months later when the priest announced that Kenneth Clark had thanked him for doing what he'd wanted for a long time. Friends were stunned and skeptical, unwilling to believe that the heart can hide its most intimate secrets.

The evidence for Clark's slow conversion is perhaps sprinkled throughout his work. In *Civilisation*, he wrote movingly of the beauty of religious imagery. He tenderly addressed iconography of the Mother of God. He explored the human need for confession, and how the modern approach to it (i.e., psychoanalysis) is full of "false turnings and dissolving perspectives."[65] He wrote:

> At this point I reveal myself in my true colors, as a stick-in-the-mud. I hold a number of beliefs that have been repudiated by the liveliest intellects of our time. I believe that order is better than chaos, creation better than destruction. I prefer gentleness to violence, forgiveness to vendetta. On the whole I think that knowledge is preferable to ignorance, and I am sure that human sympathy is more valuable than ideology. I believe that, in spite of the recent triumphs of science, men haven't changed much in the last two thousand

years; and in consequence we must still try to learn from history. History is ourselves.[66]

Clark had intuited, in his long-forgotten "moment of vision," that truth and beauty are inextricably linked, and that one may lead us to another. In the end, he realized that our yearning for beauty is our yearning for God.

Kenneth Clark died on May 21, 1983.

Notes

58. Barron, Fr. Robert. "Kenneth Clark and the Danger of Heroic Materialism." Word on Fire. http://www.wordonfire.org/Written-Word/articles-commentaries/September-2010/Kenneth-Clark-and-the-Danger-of-Heroic-Materialism.aspx.
59. Russell, John. "Kenneth Clark Is Dead at 79; Wrote 'Civilisation' TV Series." *New York Times*, May 1983.
60. Secrest, Meryle. *Kenneth Clark A Biography*. New York: Holt, Rinehart, and Winston, 1984, 27.
61. Ibid., 53.
62. Ibid., 119.
63. Ibid., 119.
64. Ibid., 232.
65. Clark, Kenneth. *Civilisation*. New York: Harper & Row, 1969, 177.
66. Ibid., 346–347.

Chapter 10

John von Neumann

December 28, 1903 – February 8, 1957

"If you gain, you gain all. If you lose, you lose nothing."[67]

— Blaise Pascal

Hungary in the early twentieth century was fertile ground for brilliance. Nobel Prize winners in medicine, chemistry, and physics sprang forth. Music, literature, and art exploded. Budapest, the fastest-growing city in Europe, boasted schools among the finest in the world. The cultural and educational boom was cranking out geniuses like a baker turns out daily bread.

Enter Fermi's Paradox. The Fermi Paradox is the question posed by Italian physicist Enrico Fermi regarding alien beings. Given a galaxy with billions of stars like the sun and earth-like planets spinning around them, the probability of intelligent life out there is high. Yet we earthlings have never made contact. "Where is everybody?" Fermi asked.

Fellow physicist Leó Szilárd replied that perhaps they are, in fact, already here. "You just call them Hungarians," he quipped.

Neumann Janos, or John von Neumann, as he was later called, was part of that pulse of Hungarian brilliance. One of the leading mathematicians of our time, his genius prompted friends and colleagues to ask a Szilárdian question: Is Johnny von Neumann really human or have the aliens landed?

Jogging Up Everest

Johnny was born to Max and Margaret, a well-to-do couple who loved and valued family and strove to provide their children with a rich home life, a robust sense of humor, inquisitiveness, and superb schooling. And though Johnny did receive a marvelous education, there were areas in which the boy barely needed to be taught, so great were his intellectual gifts. He was a pioneer in math and science: game theory, decision theory, ergodic theory, operator theory, lattice theory. He left his mark on functional analysis, cellular automata, and quantum mechanics as well as the modern computer as we know it. He worked on the Manhattan Project during World War II and developed theories of nuclear deterrence that included "Mutually Assured Destruction" (or MAD, as von Neumann dubbed it — he had an affinity for silly acronyms). It's no wonder he was part of a group of men who came to be called the Martians of science.

But even precocious children have weak areas and Johnny had his. He was not athletic; attempts to learn fencing failed. And though music and mathematics are often happy partners, Johnny did poorly with cello lessons, too. He never advanced because he propped beloved math and history books under his sheet music so he could read as he went through nothing but finger exercises on the instrument. When he entered school, he got excellent grades in all things except handwriting, physical education, and music.

He had a mathematician's mind from the time he was very young. One day when Johnny was about six years old, he saw his mother staring into space. His first thought was to ask what she was calculating. He read reams of history and retained everything for years. He could quote full chapters from Charles Dickens' novels and memorize random lists of names and numbers from the telephone book to amuse his parents' dinner guests. He was, in today's parlance, a brilliant geek. His geekiness even served him well when he used it to avoid conflict — which he avoided at all costs — in social situations. When cocktail party chatter veered into uncomfortable political debate, Johnny disarmed the situation by diverting the conversation to some obscure event from 500 B.C., on which he could easily converse for hours.

Von Neumann embodied the stereotype of the absent-minded professor. The boy who hid history books on his music stand became the man who read books while driving. The resulting accidents were much worse than a poor grade in music class. "I was proceeding down the road," he once explained. "The trees on the right were passing me in orderly fashion at sixty miles per hour. Suddenly, one of them stepped out in my path. Boom!"[68]

For one so brilliant, he made other poor judgments, too, such as the time he obtained his American driver's license by paying a shady peddler ten dollars under the Brooklyn Bridge. His second wife said that mathematics failed him only when it came to calories, and while he could recite endless pages from *A Tale of Two Cities*, he could not tell you what he had for lunch yesterday.

He published his first mathematics paper at the age of seventeen. When he headed to the university, Johnny stunned professors by proposing he work on his undergraduate and graduate degrees simultaneously. And, oh, by the way, since he had his Ph.D. project figured out, he could move ahead on that, too, if nobody minded. Biographer Norman Macrae noted, "The seventeen-year-old seemed to suggest that he would try to jog up Everest in gym shoes, although only as a part-time gig."[69] If it were anyone but von Neumann, the arrogance would have been unbelievable, but this was Johnny. Any intellectual endeavor he imagined seemed possible.

By the time he was twenty-four years old, he'd published twelve papers on mathematics. By 25, it was another ten, and by 26, the total number rose to thirty-two. Over his career, von Neumann published more than 150 papers on math and physics. His scholarly output created a near-cult among young mathematicians, reminding those of us outside the math world that their rock stars are not the same as our rock stars. They waited eagerly to see what this astounding young man would do next. Other peers felt left in the dust, wondering what they'd been doing with their lives, frittering them away on just one academic degree at a time.

The Geek Arrives

His professional life launched, it was time to think about marriage. Johnny had first met Mariette Kovesi when he was eight years old and she, age two-and-a-half, pedaled up on her tricycle to attend Johnny's younger brother's birthday party. Their childhood paths crossed regularly at their parents' summer houses. As young adults, Johnny's social awkwardness didn't immediately sweep beautiful and witty Mariette off her feet when he suggested they could have a fun life together since they both liked to drink wine. He did, however, wow her a short time later when he took a vacation with her family to Paris. He knew more about the city of love's museums than any guide book ever written, and Mariette was roundly impressed.

They got engaged in 1929. Mariette's parents approved the marriage on the condition Johnny would join the Catholic Church. Von Neumann promised he would. His mother and siblings were also converting to Catholicism at about this time, but Johnny's conversion was little more than a formality. He would go through any motion for the sake of Mariette's hand. They married in 1930, and the newlyweds left immediately for America; Johnny had been invited to teach a term at Princeton.

> Mariette's parents approved the marriage on the condition Johnny would join the Catholic Church. Von Neumann promised he would…. He would go through any motion for the sake of Mariette's hand.

Brilliant minds are not always able to channel their knowledge into effective teaching, and during his time at Princeton, Johnny wasn't known as a model instructor. He was better remembered for annoying his colleagues — including Albert Einstein — by blaring German marching songs on the gramophone in his office at the Institute for Advanced Study. His students recalled that he barely noticed their presence, complaining that von Neumann scribbled equations on the chalkboard only to erase the first and move on to the next before the baffled pupils had a chance to copy anything.

Johnny and Mariette divided their time between Princeton and Berlin. In 1935, they had their only child, Marina. A doting father, von Neumann crawled around on the floor to play with his daughter and engaged his toddler in serious discussions on subjects such as which of them was reasonably and logically entitled to the first turn with the Lincoln Logs.

Though Johnny and Mariette both adored their baby, the marriage was not thriving. Mariette, a lively, outgoing woman whose first evening jaunt in America had included checking out a speakeasy, now felt alone and neglected as a professor's wife. Johnny lived in his mind, and when entrenched in work at home, which happened often, he sometimes exploded at Mariette's interruptions, though his go-to behavior was to simply ignore his wife. In 1936, Mariette left von Neumann for another man. They divorced in 1937.

The same year Johnny became a U.S. citizen, and on a trip back to Budapest, reconnected with a childhood friend, Klari Dan, who was in the process of a divorce. She still carried a torch for her old friend Johnny and a courtship ensued. They married in 1938 and remained married until Johnny's death.

Placing His Bet

As the U.S. entered World War II, American physicist Robert Oppenheimer invited von Neumann to join the Manhattan Project, and von Neumann made significant contributions to the development of the atom bomb. Though he had concerns about its development, he conceded that it was inevitable and began exploring a nuclear deterrence theory that essentially stated that if all nations had the bomb, all nations must promise not to use it.

Johnny's work with Oppenheimer was not without personal conflict. They didn't like each other. When Oppenheimer philosophized on the chilling effect of the bomb's successful creation and quoted the *Bhagavad Gita*, intoning, "Now I am become Death, the destroyer of worlds," von Neumann had little use for the self-important drama. His response was, "Some people confess guilt to claim credit for the sin."[70]

After the war, von Neumann concentrated on computers. He pioneered much of what has become the modern computer, including his notion that a computer could have internal memory. He also accepted an appointment in 1954 from President Eisenhower as a top atomic energy commissioner. John von Neumann had built a fascinating, successful career, but one aspect of his work would exact a deadly toll.

In 1955, he began experiencing shoulder pain. X-rays showed a tumor that was initially thought to be benign. It was actually the spread of a cancer that probably began in his pancreas and had moved to his blood and into his bones; it was almost undoubtedly from radiation exposure. He was officially diagnosed in August. By November, he was incapacitated and in need of a wheelchair. In January of 1956, he was hospitalized. He left the hospital to accept a special Medal of Freedom from President Eisenhower, but he would never again leave the wheelchair.

During one hospitalization, guards were stationed outside Johnny's room to ensure that military secrets remained secret — the famous scientist was known for talking in his sleep. He sometimes hallucinated, or shouted out in Hungarian, and these nocturnal rants were possibly the seed of rumors that Johnny was screaming on his deathbed. Though he didn't scream in fear, von Neumann admitted to intimates that he sometimes gave in to despair over his impending death.

Johnny met numerous times during various hospitalizations with a Catholic priest, engaging in discussion and receiving instruction. Friends speculated it meant nothing to the agnostic. They assumed he simply enjoyed the company of a highly educated man who could converse on classical topics. But Johnny confided to his mother at one point, "There probably is a God. Many things are easier to explain if there is than if there isn't."[71] He joked about Pascal's Wager, the proposition of philosopher Blaise Pascal that it is wise to live as if there is a God, because if there is not, one hasn't lost anything. But if God exists, one has gained heaven and skirted hell.

Near the end, von Neumann amazed a visiting friend when he uttered, in perfect Latin, a saying that translated to, "When the

Judge His seat hath taken.... What shall wretched I then plead? Who for me shall intercede when the righteous scarce is freed?"[72]

Johnny received last rites and died on February 8, 1957. He was buried in Princeton cemetery, next to his mother, Margaret, who had died of cancer just a few months before Johnny's death.

Some of Johnny's friends, and even the priest who instructed him, wondered if the scientist received any comfort from his conversion. He was afraid of death until the end and seemed not to gain peace even from the sacraments. Yet fear doesn't negate faith, and belief and terror can coexist. "There probably is a God," Johnny had said, and his genius proved not the existence of aliens but the brilliance of that God who designed such a mind and universe. In the end, von Neumann placed the safest bet, trusting that his wager would pay off.

Notes

67. Pascal, Blaise. "Pascal's Pensees." Project Gutenberg. 1969. http://www.gutenberg.org/files/18269/18269-h/18269-h.htm.
68. Institute for Advanced Study. "John von Neumann's Legacy." http://www.ias.edu/people/vonneumann/legacy.
69. Macrae, Norman. *John von Neumann*. New York: Pantheon Books, 1992, 87.
70. Ibid., 245.
71. Ibid., 379.
72. Ibid., 379.

Chapter 11

Aubrey Beardsley

August 21, 1872 – March 16, 1898

"At last the door is thrown open, and all the warmth
of kind hospitality makes glad the frozen traveller."[73]
— Aubrey Beardsley

Oscar Wilde, master of mischief, malevolence, and ego, once
claimed to have invented artist Aubrey Beardsley. Initially impressed
with Beardsley's work, Wilde was no longer enamored after the two
men collaborated on an edition of Wilde's play, *Salome*. Wilde de-
nounced Beardsley's illustrations, which he considered too strongly
influenced by Japanese styles (he rather saw his play as Byzantine).
Whether Wilde found Beardsley to be incompetent or competition
is debatable, but best friends they would never be. "Beardsley's art,"
Wilde later said, was "cruel and evil and so like dear Aubrey, who
has a face like a silver hatchet and grass-green hair."[74]

If Wilde's description conjures an unpleasant image, Beardsley may have reveled in it. He delighted in the grotesque, or at least
purported to. By all accounts a sweet and courteous man, he was
also an aspirant to the decadent movement. He may have deliberately fueled the fires of competition, pushing boundaries with his
fellow aesthetes, creating art that would shock and rattle the masses
out of their typical artistic experience. A gangly man with a beak-
like nose, severe bowl haircut, and a penchant for yellow gloves,
Aubrey was anything but typical. Of his reputation as a dandy and
his poor health (he suffered from chronically weak lungs from the
age of seven) he once said, "I'm so affected that even my lungs are
affected."[75]

The Day-Job Fails to Satisfy

Born in Brighton, England, in 1872, Beardsley early displayed the temperament of an artist. He had musical talent but couldn't meet the physical demands of concerts due to his health, so he turned his attention to drawing and reading. At age twelve, when he and his sister Mabel were sent to live with an aging, cheerless aunt, he immersed himself in studying and writing about history. The following year, when he attended boarding school in Brighton, his housemaster encouraged artistic pursuits. Aubrey developed an interest in acting and wrote plays and sketches, which he and Mabel regularly performed. From his earliest days, Aubrey displayed a vibrant, active imagination and a wide array of artistic talents.

Despite evidence of outstanding talent, though, Beardsley — perhaps like so many with artistic gifts and not a clue about how to earn a living from them — took a clerical job. At the age of sixteen, he worked first in a surveyor's office and then for an insurance company. While shuffling office paper, he met a bookseller named F.H. Evans, who spotted in Beardsley an extraordinary artist with a unique vision. Evans bartered books for Beardsley's drawings. He reproduced some of them, offering them for sale, thus publicizing the young man's work. Evans' assistance was the kindling that could ignite a promising career, but then Beardsley suffered a lung hemorrhage. He was so sick for the next year and a half that he barely drew a thing.

In time, as Beardsley's health returned so did his spark. He dreamed of art school but despaired of affording it. He worried he would always be just a clerk with hidden ambitions. But artistic drive prevailed. One steamy day in July, Aubrey and Mabel went to tour the studio of Sir Edward Burne-Jones, a highly influential painter. When they arrived, they were turned away with the explanation that one needed a special appointment to gain admittance. Dejected, they shuffled off, only to be stopped by a kind gentleman who urged them to come back. "I couldn't think of letting you go away without seeing the pictures," the man said, "after a journey on a hot day like this."[76] It was Burne-Jones himself, who took them into the studio and showed them everything.

Aubrey "just happened" to have his portfolio with him, and he asked his idol if he would take a look. The meeting was life-changing. Burne-Jones was stunned by Beardsley's raw talent, and he proclaimed his drawings to be "*full* of thought, poetry, and imagination."[77] He vowed to get him into an excellent art school and asked to check in with him every three to six months. He assured Aubrey that he rarely advised anyone to pursue art as a profession — it was too tentative and unreliable — but that in Beardsley's case any other course was unthinkable. Mabel and Aubrey were then invited to join Burne-Jones and his wife for tea and to meet some other guests. "We came home with the Oscar Wildes — charming people," Aubrey wrote to his old school master.[78]

He enrolled in the Westminster School of Art and attended night classes for about a year, the only professional training he ever received. Professor Frederick Brown arranged for an exhibit of Beardsley's artwork, and Aubrey soon became a star and was sought after for professional work. He cemented his style when he illustrated an intricate new edition of Malory's *Le Morte d'Arthur*. The Malory book required working with line blocks, which limited the use of color and varying tones. An innovative and arresting black-and-white style emerged from these limitations. It would become Beardsley's trademark and lay the groundwork for the development of the Art Nouveau style. His work became immediately recognizable: black-haired beauties with simple but elegant faces, sweeping, swirling black skirts, clouds of white behind the bold silhouettes. And, too often for the taste of many, perverse or erotic imagery prevailed, especially the exaggeration of genitalia. By age twenty, Aubrey Beardsley was no longer a spiritless clerk with secret dreams but a professional artist, earning his living doing the work he loved most.

Weathering the Storm

He bought a house, and Mabel threw weekly tea parties for notables of the neighborhood, such as Robert Ross (a lifelong friend of Oscar Wilde's and the Catholic who stuck with Wilde until the end), Max Beerbohm, and Joseph Pennell. Two regular guests at tea, John Lane and Henry Harland, joined forces with Beardsley on their biggest project to date. The three had often discussed a new kind of literary magazine; it was time to launch it.

The Yellow Book, as it was called, would feature stand-alone art from Aubrey, chief art editor, in contrast to the standard approach of using drawings only to illustrate an accompanying text. The magazine would also include randomly selected stories and poetry, offering no hint of a unifying theme. In other words, *The Yellow Book* was to be another specimen of "art for art's sake," the rallying cry of the decadent movement.

Critics hated *The Yellow Book*, but their outrage didn't quell consumer response. Readers and art lovers inhaled the new sensibility deeply, and artists everywhere began to imitate Beardsley's style. Though Aubrey Beardsley was undeniably famous, he remained the kind and humble young man he'd been before the overwhelming attention.

His meteoric rise came to a screeching halt when debris from the Oscar Wilde arrest and explosion rained down around him. Aubrey's professional associations with Wilde put him in a precarious position. When Oscar Wilde was tried and jailed for sodomy, the publishers of *The Yellow Book* were nervous. Lane worried that Beardsley's collaboration with Wilde left him guilty by association, so he dismissed Beardsley from the magazine. He soon regretted it and tried to throw some work Beardsley's way, but the damage was done. No one wanted to hire Aubrey, and the rumor mill was busily grinding.

Around this time, Beardsley had the great good fortune to meet Marc Andre Raffalovich. A wealthy art patron from Paris, Raffalovich had moved to London and wanted to support Beardsley's work. The arrangement was a satisfactory one. The only concession on Beardsley's part was that he honored Raffalovich's pompous request to be addressed as "Mentor." (The pomposity would fade as the two became close friends.) Beardsley then met Leonard

Smithers, a publisher who was willing to buck the current backlash against *The Yellow Book*. Smithers partnered with Beardsley and Arthur Symons to start *The Savoy*, a similar magazine. It was less commercially successful, but more critically so. Beardsley's talent had only grown with time.

He was, however, often ill and growing more so. He was a tremendous workaholic, a habit that did not bolster his health. Some have speculated that Beardsley never dated or married because he was a homosexual, but his orientation is not definitively known. Beardsley's friend Raffalovich, however, was an admitted homosexual who converted to Catholicism in 1896. Raffalovich was in love with a poet named John Gray, who had also converted to Catholicism and gone on to become a priest. Raffalovich and Gray remained close, but chaste, and both of these friends of Aubrey's were probably influences on his slowly dawning interest in the Catholic faith. Another may have been Robbie Ross, the mutual friend of Oscar Wilde's. Almost certainly Beardsley's physical suffering was its own kind of mentor, suffering leading, as it often does, to rumination.

In the Presence of the Real Thing
In July of 1896, Beardsley took a trip to Bournemouth and stumbled on a Jesuit church that charmed him. He met Fr. David Bearne, a convert who'd been ordained just a year before meeting Beardsley. A friendship blossomed. Aubrey was genuinely moved and surprised by the interest Fr. Bearne and other Catholic friends took in him. In a letter to Raffalovich, Aubrey referred to a mutual friend whom Raffalovich had mentioned was praying for Beardsley. "I am touched to think of his childish prayers for me. I hope someday I shall have the pleasure of meeting my little beadsman," he wrote.[79]

Fr. Bearne and Beardsley spoke often, and the priest gave Beardsley books such as *A Manual of Catholic Belief*. "Fr. B.," as Beardsley referred to him in letters, was also helpful to his new friend in the frequent times of illness that Aubrey knew all too well. Aubrey was deeply touched by the priest's guileless attention.

Raffalovich, too, began sharing books about the Catholic faith with Beardsley, who promised to read them carefully then eagerly devoured them. He wrote of his fear that he was ill-equipped for the debates about Catholicism, or the "fray controversial" into which one "is sometimes forced to enter."[80] Like many converts before and after him, Beardsley undoubtedly had to deal with the opinions of friends that ranged from startled to annoyed by his interest in Catholicism.

Beardsley continued to work as much as his illness would allow. His letters are a fascinating record of the last two years of his life. On one hand, we see friendly, familiar notes such as those to Smithers, Aubrey's publisher, and Symons, the writer at *The Savoy*. In these, we see the professional young man who is trying to maintain normalcy and consistency in his work. On the flip side, we are privy to his intimate and poignant admissions to Andre that he is inching closer to faith.

Symons was one of those in "the fray controversial" who struggled to accept the spiritual side of Beardsley. In *The Art of Aubrey Beardsley*, he wrote:

> It was on the balcony of the Hotel Henri IV, at Arqus, one of those September evenings, that I had the only quite serious, almost solemn, conversation I ever had with Beardsley ... he told me then a singular dream or vision that he had had when a child, waking up at night in the moonlight and seeing a great crucifix. It is only by remembering that one conversation, that vision, the tone of awe with which he told it, that I can, with a great effort, imagine to myself the Beardsley whom I knew with his so positive intelligence, his imaginative sight of the very spirit of man as a thing of definite outline, transformed finally into the Beardsley who died in the peace of the last sacraments of the Church, holding the rosary between his fingers.[81]

This is a vital point as we ponder late life conversions. Beardsley knew Symons for most of his professional life, yet had it not been for this one conversation, Symons, who didn't see the hidden signals of a burgeoning faith, might not have believed that Beardsley had a conversion at all. Beardsley kept his longings and thoughts private, as do so many who undergo such a radical change. In those cases wherein family and friends say, "Impossible! He never spoke to me of such things!" conversion is a process that happens slowly, often invisibly, like a child growing in the womb. It is often only in hindsight that our eyes are opened. Symons continued:

> "I feel ... like someone who has been standing waiting on the doorstep of a house upon a cold day, and who cannot make up his mind to knock."

> And yet if you read carefully the book of letters to an unnamed friend, which has been published six years after his death, it will be seen here too, as always, we are in the presence of a real thing. In these naked letters we see a man die.... The whole book is a study in fear.... That he should be so honest with his fear; that he should sit down before its face and study it feature by feature; that he should never turn aside his eyes for more than an instant, make no attempt to escape, but sit at home with it, travel with it, see it in his mirror, taste it with the sacrament; that is the marvelous thing, and the sign of his fundamental sincerity in life and art.[82]

The Door Thrown Open

The final letters of Aubrey Beardsley to Andre Raffalovich are full of touching words on faith and comprise the anatomy of a conversion. We witness Beardsley's interest piqued, learn that he is visited by a kind priest, a beacon of Christ's light, and that he studies, learns, gives assent. On March 31, 1897, Aubrey made his first confession and was received into the Church by Fr. Bearne. Too ill to receive his first Holy Communion that day, he anticipated receiving Christ in the Eucharist a few days later when the Blessed Sacrament would be brought to him. He wrote to Andre, "This has been a very dry account of what has been the most important step in my life, but you will understand fully what those simple statements mean."[83]

On April 2, he wrote:

The Blessed Sacrament was brought to me here this morning. It was a moment of profound joy, of gratitude and emotion. I gave myself up entirely to feelings of happiness, and even the knowledge of my own unworthiness only seemed to add fuel to the flames that warmed and illuminated my heart. Oh how earnestly I have prayed that the flame may never die out!

My dear Andre, I understand now so much you have written to me that seemed difficult before. Through all eternity I shall be unspeakably grateful to you for your brotherly concern for my spiritual advancement.[84]

And finally this:

I feel now, dear Andre, like someone who has been standing waiting on the doorstep of a house upon a cold day, and who cannot make up his mind to knock for a long while. At last the door is thrown open and all the warmth of kind hospitality makes glad the frozen traveler.[85]

A year after his reception into the Church, Beardsley knew that he did not have much longer to live. On March 7, 1898, he wrote a letter to Leonard Smithers with the heading, "Jesus is our Lord and Judge." He wrote:

Dear Friend,

I implore you to destroy ALL copies of *Lysistrata* and bad drawings. Show this to Pollitt and conjure him to do the same. By all that is holy — ALL obscene drawings.

Aubrey Beardsley

In my death agony.[86]

Smithers, knowing that all of Beardsley's drawings would become extraordinarily valuable, did not honor the dying man's final impassioned plea. The drawings survived.

On March 12, Aubrey's sister Mabel wrote to Robbie Ross saying that she feared Aubrey would not live many more hours. He was patiently waiting, she said, ready for eternal rest. "He holds always his crucifix and rosary," she wrote.[87]

To read a man's personal letters is to enter into unguarded thoughts and intimate musings, as we do in *The Letters of Aubrey Beardsley*. From the earliest, in which seven-year-old Aubrey scribbled to his sister, "Thank you for your letter. We have pudding every day,"[88] to the final, poignant epistles that proclaim his love for Jesus Christ, we are on a journey to the truth with a young man. We see him experience his earliest glimpse of the Divine in the inherent beauty of art and music, and we watch the blossoming of hope and faith that led to a profound and sincere conversion to Christ.

On March 16, 1898, at the age of twenty-five, Aubrey Beardsley died of tuberculosis. He was in a state of grace, in love with our Lord, and in communion with the holy Catholic Church.

Notes

73. Maas, Henry, J.L. Duncan, and W.G. Good, eds. *The Letters of Aubrey Beardsley*. Oxford: Plantin Paperbacks, 1990, 290.
74. Fletcher, Ian. *Aubrey Beardsley*. Boston: Twayne Publishers, 1987, 12.
75. Fletcher, Ian. "In Black and White The Literary Remains of Aubrey Beardsley." Cypherpress. 1987. http://www.cypherpress.com/beardsley/prose/tabletalk.asp.
76. Maas, Henry, J.L. Duncan, and W.G. Good, eds. *The Letters of Aubrey Beardsley*. Oxford: Plantin Paperbacks, 1990, 22.
77. Ibid., 22.
78. Ibid., 22.
79. Ibid., 257.
80. Ibid., 262.

81. Symons, Arthur. *The Art of Aubrey Beardsley*. New York: Archive.org, 2012.   http://archive.org/stream/TheArtOfAubreyBeardsley/beards ley_aubrey_1872_1898_art_of_aubrey_beardsley_djvu.txt.

82. Ibid.

83. Maas, Henry, J.L. Duncan, and W.G. Good, eds. *The Letters of Aubrey Beardsley*. Oxford: Plantin Paperbacks, 1990, 288.

84. Ibid., 291.

85. Ibid., 290.

86. Ibid., 439. A scan of this original letter can be found at http://archive .org/stream/lastlettersofaub00bearuoft#page/156/mode/2up.

87. Ibid., 439.

88. Ibid., 7.

CHAPTER 12

Heywood Broun

December 7, 1888 – December 18, 1939

"For truth there is no deadline."[89]
— Heywood Broun

The Algonquin Round Table, a group of New York literati so famous for their biting wit that they were also called "The Vicious Circle," met at the Algonquin Hotel every day for lunch in the 1920s. According to the hotel manager's daughter, the group landed at the Algonquin "the way lightning strikes a tree, by accident and mutual attraction."[90]

The same may be true of the events that shaped Heywood Broun's life. A Round Table regular, Broun was a dazzling constellation of passions: journalist, war correspondent, sportswriter, drama critic, editor, gin aficionado, gambler, hypochondriac, the founder of the American Newspaper Guild, widely syndicated columnist, and an advocate for social issues, labor, and underdogs.

He was a radical idealist who once ran for Congress on the Socialist ticket and was eternally on the lookout for an authentic system of authority that could bring peace and fairness to an unjust world. In the end, he found the peace he longed for in a place he never predicted he would land: the Catholic Church.

Long before he had an inkling he would need or want Christianity, he rubbed shoulders with the best and brightest on literary and theatrical fronts. Broun's Algonquin lunch companions included playwright and director George S. Kaufman, *New Yorker* magazine editor Harold Ross, critic Alexander Woollcott, Harpo Marx, and the brilliant and acid-tongued writer Dorothy Parker, who purportedly quipped that she would love to engage in a battle of wits, but hated to fight an unarmed man.

One evening, Broun and Parker were at a restaurant and had an altercation with Joseph Brooks, a wealthy New Yorker with newspaper connections whom Parker must have mistaken for one unarmed. Brooks had verbally attacked Parker, so her pal Heywood took him on in a fistfight. Heywood lost. Later that night, Heywood and Dorothy discovered that Broun and Brooks had accidentally taken one another's coats after the fight. In Brooks' coat pocket was a juicy address book, brimming with irreplaceable contacts. Broun and Parker gleefully tore pages from the book and sent them fluttering, one by one, like so many rose petals out the window to the sidewalk below.

A Walking Contradiction

Heywood Broun was a rumpled Renaissance man, a sloppy gentleman full of contradictions. It was said he looked like an unmade bed, and he was once mistaken for a panhandler outside the Algonquin; a kindhearted passerby tossed a dime his way. But under the mussed exterior was a sharp intellect and a compassionate heart. Heywood Broun spent his whole life trying to reconcile his mind to his heart, his reason to a sense of faith, and his stylish friends to his frumpiness.

The frump became one of his trademarks. A *Life* magazine article from 1939 opens with a photograph of Broun sprawled on a bed reading a newspaper. "The Broun sprawl," crows the caption, "is a triumph of sheer sprawliness. His hair is uncombed, and he wears his favorite regalia: an open-neck shirt, a soft wool sweater (with holes), no socks, and an antique pair of shoes without laces." Another photo declares, "Broun, aged five, was a little Lord Fauntleroy. This is the last picture in which his pants are pressed."[91]

The sprawl did not appear to have come to him through genetics. Broun's parents were an upper-middle-class couple in New York who ran a successful printing and stationery company. He had a happy and privileged childhood, traveling to Europe with his mother before he'd reached the age of seven. He attended a private school and was intelligent, affable, and received outstanding grades in everything except German. Heywood's struggles with German drove a frustrated and volatile instructor to lob an inkpot at the boy. Broun would continue to exasperate people for the rest of his life.

Heywood's early education prepared him well, at least in the minds of his parents, for moving on to a prestigious university. He went to Harvard, but left without a degree after another foreign language debacle, flunking French class. A Harvard degree was less attractive to Broun than scratching the writing itch he'd had since the age of fourteen. He started work as a sports editor for the *New York Morning Telegraph*, commonly considered the lowest of entry level newspaper work, but was fired after two years, just when he had worked up the courage to request a raise.

He moved on to the *New York Tribune*, in the humble position of copyreader, and worked his way into every role from reporter and Sunday magazine editor, to drama critic, to book reviewer, and columnist. Broun eventually became a serious political writer and determined champion of underdogs and labor issues. His column, "It Seems to Me," was read by millions.

Broun ran for Congress in 1930 on the Socialist ticket and, while his Socialist leanings were genuine, Broun's candidacy might remind us a bit of comedian Stephen Colbert's 2008 presidential bid. Broun told someone with a straight face that he had lost all his campaign funds at a poker game. Among his high profile supporters were a couple of the Marx Brothers who, along with other Broun campaign committee members such as Dorothy Parker and Alexander Woollcott, admitted on election day that they could not vote for their beloved candidate, as they had neglected to register to vote.

After later siding with members of the Communist party who rallied for the release of the Scottsboro Nine, Broun resigned from the Socialist party. While his beliefs and convictions were sincere (he was easily left of Socialism), he often made public explanations with at least a little bit of tongue in cheek: he had not officially joined the Communist party "partly because he feels that as a Communist he would be required to make even more speeches than he likes to make."[92]

Broun's interest in labor rights led him to the founding of the American Newspaper Guild. He was its first president, traveling often to speak in support of the guild and other labor movements. Once, when addressing the United Mine Workers, his dislike of lengthy speeches was apparent. He spoke for a mere twelve minutes and sat down. The room was silent until a friend pulled Broun aside and explained that among the coal workers lengthy speeches were the norm. Speakers generally spent the first fifteen minutes, Broun's friend patiently explained, introducing themselves and pounding home the point that they were in solidarity with the movement, and during this opening spiel it was understood that nobody was listening. Broun had wrapped up his speech just as the audience was ready for him to get rolling.

In 1938, Broun started his own weekly tabloid, *The Connecticut Nutmeg*. Given that his union activities did not please his boss, Roy Howard of Scripps-Howard News Service, it's possible that Broun was looking ahead to self-employment, greater self-sufficiency, and the freedom to say and do as he liked, though he never seemed to hesitate to say and do as he liked no matter who his boss was. Broun wrote for the *Nutmeg* under several pen names, sometimes denouncing the scoundrel Heywood Broun, sometimes praising the rumpled bed for his brilliance.

Whether by accident or mutual attraction, Broun eventually married. He met Ruth Hale at a baseball game when a colleague asked Heywood if she and Ruth could sit in the press box with Broun, who was reporting on the game for the *Tribune*. He reluctantly allowed the ladies into the previously male-only space. He discovered immediately that Ruth was not a typical lady. A writer, a feminist, and an activist for women's rights, Ruth challenged his calls during the game, criticized his writing techniques, and reminded him that baseball was merely a game. He was intrigued. Though he would first go through a phase of dating and being dumped by a ballerina, and Ruth may have never gotten over feeling like his second choice, Broun eventually proposed to her. They were perfectly matched intellectually, and Ruth became, in nearly every way, Broun's best friend in the world.

They married in 1917. Ruth kept her maiden name at a time when she had to fight for the legal right to do so. In 1921, she challenged the U.S. State Department and lost when they would not issue her a passport as "Ruth Hale" instead of as "Mrs. Heywood Broun." She canceled her trip abroad rather than accept their decision, and Heywood stood by her decision, canceling his travel as well.

Ruth asserted her independence throughout the marriage. She insisted that they have only one child (they had a son, Heywood Hale Broun), and she continued her activism, which took her away from home often. The marriage grew strained, and within ten years, both considered separation. Eventually, Ruth sought a divorce as a way to regain what she perceived as the loss of independence. They divorced in 1933, but remained close friends, even continuing to share their house at times, although Heywood was now dating a widow named Connie.

Ruth became sick in 1934, and Heywood was immediately at her side. He was with her when she died in the fall of that year. In the column he wrote after her death, he lamented the loss of his best friend, saying, "For seventeen years practically every word I wrote was set down with the feeling that Ruth Hale was looking over my shoulder."[93]

About a year after Ruth's death, Broun and Connie married. Broun had hesitated about remarriage when Ruth was alive; even after her death, Connie and he agreed they should wait a respectable time in Ruth's memory. Connie was a Catholic, and she set to work taming the hard-drinking journalist who regularly carried a hip flask; she was even able to neaten him up a bit. It was a happy, peaceful marriage and Heywood adopted Connie's nine-year-old daughter, Patricia, who adored him.

Despite his outward affability, there were two issues that had followed and haunted Broun all his life: a search for definitive authority (he had hoped to find it in the Socialist party, but had been disappointed) and a fear of death. In early 1939, Heywood Broun was fifty years old and again facing his questions and fears. Broun had always experienced premonitions about dying young; there had always been an urgency to his causes. Now, in his continuing search for authority, and with his wide circle of friends and acquaintances, he found himself speaking with various priests. He kept circling back — much to his surprise and far too often for his taste — to the Catholic faith.

> Despite his outward affability, there were two issues that had followed and haunted Broun all his life: a search for definitive authority ... and a fear of death.

In February of 1939, Heywood and Connie took a trip to the southwest to look into housing conditions of the poor and destitute in the area. A priest they met there convinced Heywood that the Catholic Church shared his serious concern for the underprivileged. On the way home, during a stop in St. Louis, Broun spoke with his friend, Fr. Edward Dowling. He asked the priest if an old radical like him could find a place in the Catholic Church. Was it a crazy idea? Fr. Dowling startled Broun with his reply that the doctrines of the Church, as laid out for us by Jesus Christ, are far more radical than anything Broun had thus far imagined.

Digging Deeper

Broun interrogated other friends. One night, he cornered his life-long friend Morris Ernst, who was Jewish, and said he needed to talk, "for no less than two hours and no more than twenty."[94] He asked Ernst every question he could think of about the shocking conversion he was considering. He wondered if people would presume his wife made him do it, or if they'd think he "got religion" because of his hypochondria and fear of death. As they talked through the night, Ernst saw that Broun was profoundly sincere. His staunchest reason for conversion was that he felt a powerful pull toward the Church, and was drawn to her teaching authority. Ernst advised his friend to convert.

Sources vary about who initiated the next encounter. Some say the famous Venerable Archbishop Fulton Sheen set out to convert a famous radical. Others say that Broun sought out the Archbishop. However they connected, Heywood underwent extensive catechetical instruction from Sheen, and on May 23, 1939, Broun was baptized and confirmed by Archbishop Francis Spellman. He received his first Holy Communion at St. Patrick's Cathedral in New York.

About six months after his reception into the Church, Broun caught a cold. Within a couple of weeks, the cold turned into pneumonia, and he was hospitalized. On December 17, Sheen administered the last sacraments. Then, for a few hours, it looked as if Broun would bounce back. He told the doctor that if he lived, he'd remember what writer Ring Lardner had said, that he "would have lived longer if he had only written what he really wanted to write. And I will write only about horse racing, night clubs, gambling, and life."[95] The next day, Broun's temperature soared to 107 degrees, and on December 18, 1939, at the age of fifty-one, Heywood Broun died.

His funeral was a testament to the lives he had affected. More than three thousand mourners — proletarians, politicians, publishers, athletes, actors, waiters, writers, and ex-cons — packed into the funeral Mass at St. Patrick's Cathedral. Archbishop Sheen delivered the eulogy.

When news of Broun's conversion had first become public, a number of friends, colleagues, and readers were stunned and horrified. But Broun refused to explain himself. He wrote that

> under the obligation of a daily or weekly deadline, it is not always easy to put down with simple dignity your feelings about something that is dear to you. Very many begin, "Of course a man's religion is his own business, but...." And the

conjunction is used as a dull blunt instrument with which to club me on the head.[96]

It seemed to the man who wrote "It Seems to Me" that he owed no one an apology or an explanation for his newfound faith. He had finally found something — through accident, mutual attraction, and the mystery of grace — that he'd been searching for all his life.

Notes

89. Nelson, Harold, and Lynn Quitman Troyka. *Simon & Schuster Quick Access Reference for Writers.* Upper Saddle River, NJ: Prentice Hall, 1998, 34.

90. O'Connor, Richard. *Heywood Broun: A Biography.* New York: G.P. Putnam's Sons, 1975, 101.

91. Hellman, Geoffrey T. "Heywood Broun." *Life*, March 1939. http://books.google.com/books?id=lU0EAAAAMBAJ&pg=PA33&lpg=PA33&dq=heywood+broun&source=bl&ots=08FlXupk-h&sig=qp_nZNqUbnqn4yvaYE-HRWxGxEo&hl=en&sa=X&ei=vOBAUOfeD8rO2wW0mYDYDA&ved=0CE0Q6AEwBjgU#v=onepag.

92. Ibid.

93. O'Connor, Richard. *Heywood Broun A Biography.* New York: G.P. Putnam's Sons, 1975, 194.

94. Ibid., 212.

95. Ibid., 224.

96. Ibid., 213–14.

CHAPTER 13

Patricia Neal

January 20, 1926 – August 8, 2010

"Oh, yes, I want to be Catholic, but not yet."[97]
— Patricia Neal

On a crisp October day, a tall, striking young actress opened a grimy door and entered a rundown office building in Los Angeles. The man she loved waited for her in his car. He would be there when she emerged. She'd told him not to accompany her inside, that perhaps he should not even have driven her. At the same time, she harbored a desperate, hidden wish that he would insist on being at her side.

Her lover was twenty-five years her senior, married, and a famous actor. She would do this — have the abortion — for him. It would preserve his career, and hers, too, she reasoned. Besides, her mom might disown her if she became an unwed mother. Patricia Neal decided she would allow Gary Cooper's baby to be quietly swept from their lives. To keep their relationship alive, she would let their child, and her dream of having a family with Cooper, die.

A young doctor accepted the cash that Cooper had given Pat. She lay down on the single piece of furniture in the dingy room, an examining table, and then endured the worst hour of her life. A long needle, pain, a scraping sound. She staggered out of the building when it was over, back to Gary's car, shocked by her reentry into the normalcy of the crisp and sunny autumn day. Cooper sat in his car, sweating. He took her home and they lay on the floor of her apartment, holding each other and weeping.

Just a few days before, she had hoped this mess would end differently. The night Pat told Gary she was pregnant, she fantasized briefly about what she knew in her heart was impossible. She fancied that he, too, had a moment of wishing, wanting to have the baby they had created. He loved her; she was sure of that. She believed that they shared, for one night, the wonder of creating a life together. But the next morning, it all changed. Cooper suggested that they have things taken care of; Neal numbly agreed. The abortion would haunt her for the rest of her life. In her autobiography, *As I Am*, she wrote:

> But for over thirty years, alone, in the night, I cried. For years and years I cried over that baby. And whenever I had too much to drink, I would remember that I had not allowed him to exist. I admired Ingrid Bergman for having her son. She had guts. I did not. And I regret it with all my heart. If I had only one thing to do over in my life, I would have that baby.[98]

Neal eventually became a vocal pro-life advocate, but that transformation would not come for many years.

Passionate Ambition

When she was ten years old, Patsy Louise Neal sat in the basement of the Methodist church in Knoxville, Tennessee. Her teacher, Miss Cornelia Avaniti, delivered a dramatic monologue; the little girl in the audience was mesmerized. At that moment, she knew what she wanted to be. "Dear Santa," she wrote when she got home that night, "What I want for Christmas is to study dramatics. Please."[99] Moving to New York City became her mission.

At nineteen, she moved to Manhattan and changed her name to Patricia at the suggestion of a director (though friends still called her Pat). She quickly found success on Broadway, winning a Tony Award for her role in Lillian Hellman's *Another Part of the Forest* in 1947. Capitalizing on her stage success, the sultry, husky-voiced actress moved to Hollywood. She immediately landed a role opposite Ronald Reagan and then met the man who held an iron grip on her heart for years. The attraction between Patricia Neal and Gary Cooper simmered as they were filming *The Fountainhead*. Their affair, perhaps the only one that ever really threatened Cooper's marriage, boiled over as soon as the movie was finished.

Their liaison lasted several years, but after the abortion, Cooper told his wife everything. Pat was stunned and distressed, but grateful for the immediate fallout: he moved out of his home, and their relationship continued. Only in retrospect did she understand Cooper's revelation to his wife to be a sign of impending doom. Gary wouldn't have confessed everything to Veronica if he didn't somehow plan to start over with her. It was only a matter of time, but Neal blinded herself to that truth.

Gossip rags now regularly badgered Neal regarding her appearances in public with Cooper. Maria, Gary Cooper's young daughter, saw her father's mistress one day and spat at her. Reporters followed Pat to work on the set of the science fiction film *The Day the Earth Stood Still*. Her costar, Michael Rennie, teased that she should respond to their questions about her homewrecker status with a line from the movie: "Klaatu barada nikto!"

One night, after Gary and Pat arrived at a party, Mrs. Cooper swept in on the arm of actor Peter Lawford. Neal had already been having a bad day — she felt dowdy that night, inappropriately dressed. Why had she put those silly flowers in her hair, she wondered. Veronica, on the other hand, looked polished, stunning. When someone else asked Neal to dance, Cooper approached Veronica. Pat finished the dance, returned to the table, and watched her lover and his wife sway together on the dance floor. The agony of another awful time she'd been left alone pierced her. That dingy office on that October day…. She felt alone, always alone. When Gary returned to their table, she insisted he take her home. She hoped he would stay the night, but he begged off, saying he felt ill, and besides, he had an early flight to New York. He left. She was alone again.

A Bitter End

"Coop's in the hospital."[100]

A mutual friend called to deliver the news. An ulcer. Pat concluded it was because he held everything inside, that he was slowly killing himself with their secrets. She called and begged him to allow her to visit the hospital, but he refused. Desperate and fearing she was being shut out, Neal called Cooper's mother, Alice, to enlist her help. She needed an ally. But Alice delivered a mortal emotional blow. "He is sick," she told Pat, "because of you."[101]

Weeping and trembling, humiliated because her lover would not commit to her, and desolate because she could never have a family with him, Neal called Cooper and ended the relationship. Just as she'd wished he'd stayed by her side for the abortion, she wished now that he would not accept her decision. But he wanly acceded. There would be a couple more false starts, but Cooper would never leave his wife, a Catholic, and he loved his daughter too dearly to subject her to divorce.

Ten years after the end of the affair, and eight years since she'd married someone else, Pat heard the news. Gary Cooper was dead, a victim of cancer. In a strange way, she felt a sort of relief. She could stop looking on every street corner for the man she really loved, cease wishing that he would return to her. She stopped in at a nearby Catholic Church and said a prayer, though she wasn't entirely sure why.

They Told Her So

"Don't marry him, Patsy! He's a horror."[102]

Dashiell Hammett didn't think much of Patricia Neal's intended. Neither did another of Patricia Neal's friends — Leonard Bernstein told her she'd be making the mistake of her life if she married him. She did it anyway. Pat wanted a family, and when the man she'd been dating assumed they would marry, she followed the course he charted. But in a hidden recess of her heart, she admitted a pathetic truth to herself. She did not love him; he was the only man she had ever chosen for an ulterior motive — motherhood.

They met at a dinner party at playwright Lillian Hellmann's home. Pat inquired about the handsome six-foot-six-inch man across the room. He was Roald Dahl, the writer whose imagination would hatch Willie Wonka, James and his giant peach, and numerous other children's books. The quintessential Renaissance man, it seemed there was nothing Dahl wouldn't tackle. He had been a pilot and intelligence officer in the Royal Air Force during World War II, and eventually would co-invent an intricate medical device that helped his infant son recover from a tragic injury. But that accomplishment was years in the future. On this night, Dahl and Neal sat next to one another at dinner, and Pat was eager to impress this intriguing gentleman. Dahl, however, did not act the part of gentleman; he deliberately ignored her during the entire meal. Furious, Neal left the party convinced he was a loathsome thing.

Dahl was nothing if not unpredictable. He surprised her with a phone call, and a request for a date. She was delighted to have the chance to spurn him. He called again, and she relented. On their first date at an Italian restaurant, he stared at her over candlelight and red wine and said with a straight face, "I would rather be dead than fat."[103] After dinner, Roald took her to a friend's penthouse and by the end of the evening, his friend advised him to drop every other female in his life and hang on to this one.

They were married in 1953 and had five children: Olivia, Tessa, Theo, Ophelia, and Lucy. Neal's dream of family life was realized, but during their marriage Pat and Roald would experience so much misfortune that their life together has been likened to a Greek tragedy.

Their son Theo was just four months old when a car struck his carriage as his nanny pushed it across the street. Theo sustained a brain injury followed by a long, laborious recovery requiring several surgeries and an enormous amount of rehabilitation. Dahl, intent on doing whatever he could to help his son, collaborated with two friends, an engineer and a neurosurgeon, to develop the Wade-Dahl-Till Valve, a shunt that successfully drained fluid from the brain.

Just two years later, their eldest child, seven-year-old Olivia, contracted measles and died. Roald, whose sister had died when she was seven and whose father passed away six weeks after that, was insane with grief, fearing an illogical connection, wondering if he, too, would soon die. Neal ministered to her husband and struggled to break through his shell. In the meantime, Theo underwent his eighth craniotomy. The Dahl family persevered, and they slowly began to recover. Pat turned to work, channeling her grief into her craft, and won an Academy Award for her role in *Hud*. Soon after, she became pregnant again, and the pledge and anticipation of new life brought healing to Pat and Roald's wounds. They named the new baby Ophelia.

Another Tragic Turn

In 1965, pregnant with their fifth child, Lucy, Pat was helping seven-year-old Tessa in the bathtub when she felt a searing pain in her left temple. She stood, stumbled into the bedroom, and told her husband she was seeing things. He asked what; she suddenly couldn't recall. As Dahl reached for the phone, Neal could think only, "I have children to care for. I have another inside me. I cannot die."[104]

She suffered a series of three strokes that left her in a coma for weeks. She finally awoke to complete paralysis on her right side, double vision, loss of speech, and an inability to process her thoughts or communicate in any coherent way.

Dahl swooped in and took total control of the household and the children. He was instrumental in Neal's recovery with his schedule of constant, grueling therapy, but he was often cruel. He pushed several hours of speech therapy a day on her when the experts recommended no more than one. When her mother visited and cooked Pat a juicy steak as a treat, Roald took it away, cut it into pieces, and doled it out to everyone, declaring his wife was not to receive special treatment. He did not think a night nurse was necessary, and when she had to use the bathroom in the middle of the night, as pregnant women frequently do, Neal never woke Dahl. She kidded herself that it was because she wanted him to rest after caring for her and the children all day. In reality she was afraid to hear him say, "No, you can do it yourself."[105]

He threw away the many cards, telegrams, and well-wishes that poured in, and he refused to show her any encouragement that bore a religious slant (though with that, Pat agreed — she hated God for what He had done to her). And though Neal sympathized with what Dahl himself must have been going through, she longed for tenderness and understanding. When he initiated sexual contact too soon, she was petrified; she described the encounter as agony.

About five and a half months after the stroke, Lucy was born. Dahl's disregard for his wife's feelings continued. Without discussing the matter with his wife, Roald ordered the doctor to perform a tubal ligation immediately after Lucy's birth. Pat submitted to his decision at the time, but years later felt outraged by his arrogance. Perhaps this additional loss of future children even brought to the surface unresolved grief from the abortion.

For all of his coldness, Roald Dahl did indeed help his wife to fully recover from the devastating strokes. And another kind of recovery had begun: in the months just after the stroke, Pat received a note from Maria Cooper. It said, simply, "I forgive you."[106]

Betrayal and Beginnings

Felicity "Liccy" Crosland, a pretty thirty-something advertising coordinator with a friendly smile and a winning personality, befriended Patricia Neal when they worked together on Pat's Maxim coffee commercial campaign in the early 1970s. The tendrils of Liccy's friendship with Pat wound their way into the entire family. The children loved her, and Felicity helped Roald with numerous domestic tasks, such as shopping for gifts for his wife. So Pat was shocked and devastated when she discovered that her friend and her husband were having an affair.

Neal sought solace in her children, in charitable endeavors with stroke victims, and in her work and travel. Once, while in New York, she invited Maria Cooper to come for breakfast. Ever since the note of forgiveness had arrived, Pat had tried to arrange a meeting. When Maria arrived, the women hugged; they spoke frankly, as adults and equals. Maria asked if it was true that there had been a pregnancy. Neal admitted it, and Maria expressed regret that she had never met her only sibling. She also asked Patricia to write to her mother, who was now remarried. They parted, but the seeds of an unlikely friendship had been planted.

In 1978, while working on a film in Europe, she ran into Maria again. As they talked that night, Neal admitted that she had been angry at God for a long time. Maria suggested spending time with some Benedictine nuns at the Abbey of Regina Laudis, in Connecticut.

Neal didn't immediately jump on the odd idea, but eventually investigated. En route to her first visit to the abbey, she stopped to buy bottles of wine and vodka, thinking she might need liquid fortification in the presence of so much holiness.

> En route to her first visit to the abbey, she stopped to buy bottles of wine and vodka, thinking she might need liquid fortification in the presence of so much holiness.

In the three days she spent with the nuns she shared their meals, performed Helen Keller's works for them, and had talks with the abbess. One day in the garden, Pat told the abbess she was sure her current round of misery was due to the struggles in her marriage. The abbess encouraged her to dig, to unearth the real reasons for her feelings. Neal poured out her story: her love for Gary Cooper, the end of their affair, her desperate longing for him. She told the abbess that his marriage had left them no way to be together. Pat was puzzled by the abbess' reply that there actually was a way, a path that Neal simply could not yet see.

Before she left, Pat picked a delicate flower. She asked if it could be left in the chapel in memory of Olivia. At evening prayer, she noticed that someone had placed the blossom in front of the altar. Deeply moved by this kindness, she went to her room and wept. At the end of her first glimpse into the Benedictine life, Pat realized she hadn't touched the alcoholic insurance she'd stowed away.

Occasional visits evolved into a routine as Pat, finding comfort there, went to the Abbey every three months. One day Pat saw an obituary in the paper: Dr. John Converse had died, survived by his wife, Veronica ("Rocky" as she was often called), the former Mrs. Gary Cooper. Neal finally wrote to Rocky, expressing her sympathy for the losses of John and Gary. Rocky's reply went beyond thanking Neal for her kindness. She wrote that Pat had surely carried her own cross, as had she. These women, who'd both survived the wreckage from their relationships with Gary Cooper, were reconciled after so many years.

Soon after that, Pat attended a service at the abbey in which they prayed for the dead. Seized by a strong desire, she announced she would become Catholic. The nuns gently suggested she consult her husband first. They encouraged her to invite him to the abbey, which Pat did, but Dahl could not have been less interested. He left Pat and began making plans to marry Felicity Crosland.

Though it had been a difficult and often unhappy marriage, Dahl had been Patricia Neal's life for thirty years. He had utterly directed her days for the last fifteen, and he was the father of her beloved children. Now she felt she had nothing. The divorce proceedings were ugly.

Pat turned to the nuns for comfort, but formal instruction was put on hold as Pat grappled with bitterness. She visited the sisters so often that one day the abbess suggested Neal live at the abbey for a month, in the manner of a pre-postulant. She accepted.

She prayed, went to Mass, weeded the garden, baked bread. The days were outwardly peaceful but inwardly seething. One day, in conversation with the abbess, Pat lost her temper. An explosion of self-pity erupted. The abbess lost her patience, too. Fed up with her guest's rants, the abbess curtly suggested Pat leave. But Neal couldn't do it. She was finally ready to accept the fundamental truth the sisters repeatedly shared with her — that there is freedom in our ability to accept the sufferings that God allows; such freedom helps us heal.

Ripe for genuine spiritual change, Neal helped the sisters decorate the Christmas tree that month and was struck in a new way by its beauty. It seemed to her something ethereal, a burning bush, a source of eternal love. That Christmas, she sensed a new understanding of the Nativity and had a powerful and mysterious sense that life was beginning anew.

The abbess had once told Pat that God sometimes asks us to accept the weight of a large suffering to get rid of a smaller one. Pat questioned the wisdom of that. Why anyone would do such a thing?

"You have to love very much," the abbess said. "You begin by remembering, Patricia. And when you remember all, what remains is love."[107]

A publisher approached Pat about writing a memoir. The abbess encouraged her to journal about her life, to make it a spiritual exercise, and if she felt that her story would help others, only then to consider a book. Pat was offered the use of a nearby house for the writing. She spent five years on her memoirs and began embracing the theme of the abbess's exhortations: "There is a way to love that remains after everything else is taken from us." Dolores Hart, a former actress who left Hollywood to join a religious order (she is now Mother Dolores), helped Pat write the 1,200 pages that eventually became her autobiography, *As I Am*. In an interview with the *National Catholic Register*, Mother Dolores said of Pat:

> When I would inquire about her faith, she kept telling me, "Oh yes, I want to be Catholic, but not yet." I would ask her, "What do you mean, not yet?" She said, "I like being Catholic when I'm here, but not when I'm not here."
>
> "That's not going to do God any good," I would reply. "He wants you to be Catholic all the time."
>
> I didn't believe in pushing her. Four months ago, when she was hospitalized with her illness, she called me and said she wanted to be a Catholic. She made the step at that time. She had waited a long time and finally threw in her towel on March 30, 2010.[108]

On August 8, 2010, four months after being received into the Catholic Church, Patricia Neal died of lung cancer. Her life of suffering had taught her to "remember all." What remained for her in the end was love. She is buried at the Abbey of Regina Laudis in Connecticut.

Notes

97. Drake, Tim. "Mother Dolores Hart Talks About Patricia Neal, Gary Cooper." *National Catholic Register*, August 25, 2010. http://www.ncregister.com/blog/tim-drake/mother-dolores-hart-talks-about-patricia-neal-gary-cooper.
98. Neal, Patricia. *As I Am*. New York: Pocket Books, 1988, 137.
99. Ibid., 29.
100. Ibid., 145.
101. Ibid., 145.
102. Ibid., 172.
103. Ibid., 161.
104. Ibid., 272.
105. Ibid., 286.
106. Ibid., 298.
107. Ibid., 396.
108. Drake, Tim. "Mother Dolores Hart Talks About Patricia Neal, Gary Cooper." *National Catholic Register*, August 25, 2010. http://www.ncregister.com/blog/tim-drake/mother-dolores-hart-talks-about-patricia-neal-gary-cooper.

CHAPTER 14

Gary Cooper

May 7, 1901 – May 13, 1961

"The only thing I can say for me is that I'm trying to be a little better."[109]

— Gary Cooper

The angelically pretty brown-haired, blue-eyed little girl's face was streaked with tears. She walked with her mother, a regally beautiful woman, and as they passed a pickup truck the girl looked hard at a woman sitting inside the vehicle. The sadness on her face twisted into anger. She spat forcefully on the ground, glaring at the woman behind the glass.

Maria Cooper, eleven years old, had just looked into the eyes of the one who — she had discovered only the night before — was her father's mistress.

Easy-Going Charisma

Gary Cooper was a popular, wildly successful actor who with devilish ease portrayed every role from the clumsy, boyish love interest in a screwball comedy, to rugged cowboy, to sophisticated-man-about-town. He appeared in nearly a hundred films from 1925 to 1961 and earned Academy Awards for two of them, *Sergeant York* and *High Noon*. The variety in his movie roles was perhaps foreshadowed by his childhood, in which he also played shy bumbler, country boy, and gentleman. Frank James Cooper (he took the name Gary later, on the advice of a casting director) was born in Montana to parents who had emigrated from England, went on to own a ranch, and worked in law and the justice system.

As a teenager, Gary seemed not to realize how good-looking he was or how his presence affected the giggling girls at school as he tripped past them. The man who eventually gained a reputation as a dapper dresser (he was immortalized in the Irving Berlin song *Puttin' on the Ritz*: "Dressed up like a million dollar trouper/Tryin' hard to look like Gary Cooper/Super Duper!") loved the outdoors, was comfortable with cattle, and handled horses with ease. But he also spent a portion of his childhood at a proper British school, at his mother Alice's insistence.

Gary Cooper was a man riddled with paradox, not the least being that although he strained against the harness of fidelity, he was a devoted father and family man who is still remembered as a genuinely loving and caring person. His daughter tells the story of Cooper making a four-hour round trip on horseback to accompany home two little boys who had come in search of their hero. And colleague George C. Scott said:

> I tell you — he was kind. We were on location in Yakima, Washington. Somebody came up to his trailer and said, "There's a couple of kids and they want your autograph." Now, I would never get out of my trailer and go down. The man got up, walked down, about a quarter of a mile, signed the autographs — I saw him come back myself — and, y'know, that was the kind of sweetness he had in his nature.[110]

Cooper was the kind of young man who didn't like to bother people, deflected attention from himself, and listened to the voice of authority. So when as a teenager, after a car accident, the doctor told him he'd merely torn hip ligaments, he didn't complain about the pain. He followed his doctor's suggestion to rest for a few days and then get on a horse for exercise, to strengthen his hip. The pain was excruciating, but Gary obeyed, spending so much time riding that he became an expert horseman. Eventually he healed and the misery subsided, but the young horseman was left with a stiff gait.

The correct diagnosis came years later when, at age forty, X-rays revealed that Cooper had actually fractured his hip in the accident.

After attending Grinnell College in Iowa, Cooper landed in California and a series of jobs followed: newspaper and advertising work, theater curtain sales, electric sign sales. His life's direction took an unexpected turn when he followed a friend's suggestion to try stunt and extra work in the movies. Frank's magnetism jumped off the screen, and the young man who'd failed to make it into the drama club at Grinnell went on to build a career of subtle but powerful, highly lauded performances on film.

The charisma that Gary Cooper exuded onscreen extended to real life — he was pursued by nearly every woman he met and indulged in affairs with many of them, from costars to socialites. But when he met Veronica "Rocky" Balfe in 1933, he had finally met his match. Rocky was smart, gorgeous, and athletic; she loved swimming, tennis, and horses. Gary Cooper fell in love.

> ... her marriage was a sacrament, and her commitment to her husband was a promise for life. She was not to be trifled with.

Rocky fell in love, too, and although twelve years younger than Cooper, was no naive ingenue. Intent on ensuring that past relationships would remain safely in the past, Rocky invited three women for tea one day, all of them Gary's former lovers. The intrepid Mrs. Cooper glanced around the table, of which she clearly had command. She then returned a few trinkets to her teatime companions, gifts they had given her husband in the past. "He won't be needing these anymore," was the stern if unspoken message.

Rocky was Catholic, her marriage was a sacrament, and her commitment to her husband was a promise for life. She was not to be trifled with.

The End of the Affair

Sixteen years into his marriage, Gary Cooper and the actress Patricia (Pat) Neal began an extended affair that might have gone undetected for much longer than it did if not for an innocent mistake made by a mutual friend.

Harvey Orkin was Gary Cooper's publicist, and Pat Neal's good friend, but he was unaware of the ongoing affair between the two. One day in July of 1949, Harvey invited himself, his girl-friend, and Pat, along with Pat's vacationing mother, to visit the Cooper family in Aspen at the construction site of their new home. Rocky and Maria flew out together, Pat's mother rode with Harvey and his girlfriend, and Pat and Gary drove together to Aspen. By the second day of the strained trip, the tangled web unraveled.

As Gary and Pat sat together in a pickup truck outside a hotel, Rocky and Maria walked by. Rocky's face was blank, unread-able, but eleven-year-old Maria had clearly been crying. When she looked through the truck window and saw Neal, Maria's sorrow turned to rage. She spat at the ground, and continued walking at her mother's side.

Pat and Gary, shaken, took a drive. "Last night," Cooper began, "Rocky asked me if I was having an affair with you. I said yes. She wanted to know if I was in love with you. I said yes. Maria came in just about then and Rocky told her everything."[111]

If Veronica Cooper's nickname did not come from the fact that she was rock solid, grounded, and strong, perhaps it should have. The night the story came out, Rocky told her daughter to go and give her father a hug, that he was extremely upset about every-thing. She assured her beloved little girl that the marital problems had nothing whatsoever to do with her and that this trouble did not alter their love for her a bit.

Cooper may have been extremely upset, but the affair con-tinued. He took Neal to Cuba to visit his friend, Ernest Heming-way. The two men had become close after Cooper appeared in films based on Hemingway's books. Hemingway was kind to Neal that weekend, but he and his wife Mary disapproved of the extramarital affair. Though Mary was Hemingway's fourth wife, Ernest believed in at least serial monogamy.

After they returned home from Cuba, Cooper did a radio play and Pat sent him a telegram, gushing over his performance. When a return message arrived, she ripped it open, eager to read her lover's response. Instead, she was shocked to see the words, "I have had just about enough of you. You had better stop now or you will be sorry. Mrs. Gary Cooper."[112]

Cooper still did not end it. It was not until after Patricia Neal's pregnancy, an abortion, and a separation from his wife that his relationship with Neal finally came to a close. Though he seemed to love Neal, he also loved his wife, and he adored his daughter. Eventually he developed an ulcer and was hospitalized; the time was ripe for making changes.

"Whatever decision making process he went through," Maria said years later, "when he decided he wanted to come back home … those are always mutual decisions, you know? It takes two. I think it's stupid to say you go back, 'cause you don't go back to anything. You either have the wherewithal to pick up and start again … and the two of them did, and as a family we did."[113]

The Best Thing I Ever Did

Rocky and Maria joined Gary on a trip to Europe in 1953, and a coveted dream of Maria's came true when the family was granted an audience with Pope Pius XII. Gary helped his wife and daughter hold the myriad rosaries and medals they had brought to be blessed, but when he genuflected, he tripped, sending beads and medals flying. Gary Cooper, American movie icon, hunched over at the feet of the pope and gathered up the scattered treasures.

Quietly, without fanfare or announcements, Cooper began going to Mass with his family. When Rocky first invited Fr. Harold Ford over for a drink one day, perhaps she hoped for a dramatic, life-changing afternoon of intense spiritual discussion between the priest and her husband. Instead, Cooper and Fr. Ford swapped hunting and fishing stories. Soon after, the priest, whom Gary started calling Fr. Tough Stuff, joined the family regularly for scuba diving expeditions. The friendship grew as the conversations continued.

Eventually, Cooper decided to take formal instruction. On April 9, 1959, he was received into the Catholic Church. Cooper expressed doubts to his friend Hemingway, but concluded that because he "believed in belief"[114] everything would probably work out. Though he was private about his faith, Cooper said this in an interview:

> "Having a faith, being a Catholic … made a big difference to me. I found out you don't have to get all wound up in religion, but the knowledge that it is there, with its rules and its vast storehouse of experience, gives you an inner security…. I'll never be anything like a saint, I know. I just haven't got that kind of fortitude. The only thing I can say for me is that I'm trying to be a little better. Maybe I'll succeed."[115]

Diagnosed with prostate cancer in 1960, Cooper had surgery to remove part of his colon. The public story was that everything was under control. In reality, by the end of the year, the cancer had spread to his lungs. By February of 1961, Gary was dying. "Every time he'd receive Communion," Rocky later told a reporter, "he said he felt so much better. He was completely unafraid of the future. He really was. No fear whatsoever."[116]

In April, Cooper was too weak to attend the Academy Awards to accept an honorary Oscar for career achievement. His close friend, Jimmy Stewart, accepted the award for him, and when Stewart nearly broke down, the gravity of Cooper's illness became public. President Kennedy sent words of encouragement and the Secretary of State of the Vatican sent a message on behalf of the pope:

> The Holy Father, fondly recalling the visit of Gary Cooper and his family, is grieved to learn of his illness and lovingly imparts a special apostolic blessing, the pledge of abundant comfort, and divine grace and favors.[117]

Within a month, death was imminent. A mutual friend of Gary and Ernest Hemingway, A.E. Hotchner, visited him near the end. As Cooper and Hotchner spoke, Cooper placed a crucifix on his pillow, near his head, and said:

> "Please give Papa [Hemingway] a message.... It's important and you mustn't forget because I'll not be talking to him again. Tell him, that time I wondered if I made the right decision —" He brought the crucifix to his cheek. "Tell him it was the best thing I ever did."[118]

Cooper's daughter, Maria, pointed out that a Trappist monk whom he had never met played an ironic role in her father's final weeks. Gary's godfather was photoessayist Shirley Burden. Shirley's book *God Is My Life: The Story of Our Lady of Gethsemani* featured a foreword from Fr. Thomas Merton, which is perhaps what prompted Cooper to read Merton's book *No Man Is an Island*, from which he derived great comfort. The monk's book shares a title with what had always been one of Cooper's favorite poems by John Donne, the lines of which he determinedly copied out just two weeks before he died:

> No man is an island entire of itself ... any man's death diminishes me, because I am involved in mankind; and therefore never send to know for whom the bell tolls; it tolls for thee.

After Cooper passed away, Maria wrote to Fr. Merton, and she received a sympathy note in return. He had loved her father's movies, he confessed, and admitted to the temptation to imagine his autobiography, *The Seven Storey Mountain*, as a film starring her father. Even Trappist monks were not immune to Gary Cooper's charm.

The last week of Cooper's life, he was on strong pain medication that left him sleeping most of the time. On Thursday, May 11, he was able to speak to a priest friend, Fr. Daniel Sullivan, and the next day he received last rites. "I know," he told Rocky near the end, "I know what is happening is God's will."[119]

On May 13, 1961, Gary Cooper died, with Rocky and Maria by his side.

Notes

109. Carpozi, Jr., George. *The Gary Cooper Story*. New Rochelle, NY: Arlington House, 1970, 210.

110. *Gary Cooper The Face of a Hero*. Janson Media. Film.

111. Neal, Patricia. *As I Am*. New York: Pocket Books, 1988, 124.

112. Ibid., 133.

113. *Gary Cooper The Face of a Hero*. Janson Media. Film.

114. Arce, Hector. *Gary Cooper An Intimate Biography*. New York: William Morrow and Company, 1979, 270.

115. Carpozi, Jr., George. *The Gary Cooper Story*. New Rochelle, NY: Arlington House, 1970, 210.

116. Ibid., 215.

117. Arce, Hector. *Gary Cooper An Intimate Biography*. New York: William Morrow and Company, 1979, 278.

118. Ibid., 279.

119. Neal, Patricia. *As I Am*. New York: Pocket Books, 1988, 403.

Afterword

Mike took a chance.

On a crisp December day, he sat at the hospital with his sixty-nine-year-old father-in-law, Harry. Harry's heart was failing; now he was battling pneumonia, too, and he had begun talking about his funeral. Mike sensed that for the first time, Harry was pondering what lay beyond. Oh, Harry hadn't actually come out and said as much — could he be embarrassed? What does a man feel so late in life when he's never dug into the stuff of God, Mike wondered. He, a cradle Catholic, and his wife, Monica, a convert, had never pushed their faith on Monica's dad; they never even discussed it.

It felt risky. But it felt right. He took the plunge. "So, um, baptism," Mike said tentatively. "Is that … something that you want?"

"Yes," replied Harry, straining to speak, but brightening. "Yes."

Mike and Monica called their friend, Fr. John, who had known Mike since childhood. The priest hurried over that Sunday afternoon, his main concern that Harry was acting of his own volition, that he genuinely desired the sacraments — it had to be Harry's choice. After asking a few questions, to which the dying man nodded assent, Fr. John was convinced this was indeed the case. The priest baptized Harry, confirmed and received him into the Catholic Church, and gave him his first Holy Communion, assuming it would also be his last. Fr. John, Mike, and Monica witnessed visible relief and happiness on Harry's face.

As it turned out, Harry's first Holy Communion was not his last. He rallied, and about a week later, when he could speak without pain, he confessed to his daughter that this should have happened long ago. He lived for a month after his baptism, and Mike and Monica encountered a changed man, one who was more talkative, more reflective, and shared his emotions easily and more often. He appeared at peace with God, with himself, and with whatever time he had left on earth. Harry died shortly after New Year's Day.

In his homily at the funeral, Fr. John shared the story of the Good Thief — the criminal crucified next to Jesus — who just before his death

> ... encounters the saving love of Jesus Christ. Preachers sometimes refer to this passage as the one where "the good thief steals heaven." It's a nice play on words, but not quite accurate — no one can "steal" heaven, no one has a right to salvation. Eternal life is a gift, freely given by a God who loves us so much that He sent His only Son to die for us. And what is it that we have to do? It's quite simple, really — accept the invitation.[120]

The same thought had struck Mike. "It was as if," Mike said, "Harry was waiting for someone to ask him."

One result of Harry's conversion was that he became a beacon. Monica's four siblings, none of whom had been raised with or had adopted religion, were stirred by the funeral Mass; they had never experienced anything like it. They thanked Monica and Mike not only for handling the practical arrangements, but for the beauty and intimacy of the Mass, this final gift to their father. One family member has since taken tentative steps to investigate the Church. Through his death, Harry spread the life of Christ. But it might not have happened, as Mike said, "if he hadn't been asked."

Getting to the Point

Fr. Ed Thompson took a chance, too, though his approach was more direct, to say the least. Bert Ghezzi tells this story about his priest friend:

> One day a nurse suggested that Fr. Thompson visit a cantankerous cancer patient who was a non-practicing Catholic.

"Hello," he said as he walked into the man's room. "I'm Fr. Ed, and I thought I'd drop in to see how you are doing."

"Get the hell out of here," said the patient, following his sharp greeting with unprintable expletives.

So Fr. Ed left. Over the next three months he tried numerous times to visit the man, but without success. "Call me immediately when he turns for the worse," he told a nurse.

A few days later she called, and he left the dinner table to rush to the dying patient's side.

"What the hell are you doing here?" asked the man.

"I thought that now you might want to set things right with God and the Church," said Fr. Ed.

"Not interested," he said. "You can just take your Bible and get out." Then he drifted off in a hazy sleep. But Fr. Ed sat down in a chair by the bed and waited.

When the man woke, he said, "What are you still doing here? I told you to leave."

"Well," said Fr. Ed, "I've never seen anyone go to hell, so I thought I'd watch you."

That did it. The man broke down crying and asked for Fr. Ed's help. Father heard his confession, anointed him, and gave him the Eucharist, which he had not received for decades. He died peacefully, reconciled to God and the Church and forgiven of all his sins.[121]

Fr. Ed may have been blunt, but he sensed something. He and the dying patient were somehow on the same wavelength, just as Mike and Harry had been.

God Ran

"Not many days later, the younger son gathered all he had and took his journey into a far country, and there he squandered his property in loose living.... But when he came to himself he said ... 'I will arise and go to my father, and I will say to him, "Father, I have sinned against heaven and before you; I am no longer worthy to be called your son; treat me as one of your hired servants."' And he arose and came to his father. But while he was yet at a distance, his father saw him and had compassion, and ran and embraced him and kissed him.... The father said to his servants, 'Bring quickly the best robe, and put it on him; and put a ring on his hand, and shoes on his feet; and bring the fatted calf and kill it, and let us eat and make merry; for this my son was dead, and is alive again; he was lost, and is found.'" (Luke 15:13–24)

Conversions are as strange and individual as the people who experience them. Some transformations, weighted with drama, are Damascus road affairs that defy reason, but others come quietly after puzzles and questions, self-conscious searching, years of private pondering. If it's true, as Oscar Wilde said, that our real lives are often the lives we don't lead, then decoding the contents of any human heart is nearly impossible. Sometimes we can't decipher our own motives and intentions, surely we can't figure out everyone else's. The good news is we don't have to. Happily, God handles the who, what, when, where, and why of salvation. What a relief.

One final story. In "The Repentant Sinner," Russian writer Leo Tolstoy told of a seventy-year-old man who, on his deathbed, cried out to God for the pardon that had been shown the Good Thief. The man had been a hardened sinner all his life and when he died he found himself at the gates of heaven. He knocked and an unseen accuser on the other side recounted all the man's evil deeds, unable to note a single kind or noble act. He ordered the man to depart. The sinner asked the gatekeeper's name and discovered it was St. Peter. He begged Peter to have pity — he, the sinner, was just the same as Peter, who had denied Christ.

Peter fell silent.

The sinner tried again, and discovered that King David was now on the other side of the gate. He again begged pardon, saying that just as David had been guilty of adultery and murder, so too had he, but just as David had prayed, "I acknowledge my transgressions: my sin is ever before me," so did this sinner acknowledge his crimes before God.

David fell silent.

When the man tried a third time, another voice told him to go away, because evildoers could never enter heaven. The man discovered he was now talking to John, the beloved disciple of Jesus and he exulted and said:

> Peter and David must let me in, because they know man's weakness and God's mercy; you must let me because you love much. You wrote that God is Love, that he who loves not, knows not God. You said, "Love one another." How, then, can you look on me with hatred, and drive me away? Either you must renounce what you said or, loving me, must let me enter the kingdom of heaven.[122]

John opened the gate.

Another prodigal son was home.

Notes

120. Homily, from Fr. John.

121. Adapted from *Living the Sacraments: Grace into Action*, Bert Ghezzi (Cincinnati, Ohio: Servant Books), 2011.

122. Tolstoy, Leo. *Twenty-Three Tales*. N.p.: Gutenberg Consortia Center http://ebooks.gutenberg.us/WorldeBookLibrary.com/23tales. htm#1_5_6 (I have paraphrased these lines in modern language).

Acknowledgments

I am indebted, as always, to my marvelous editor, Cindy Cavnar, who pushes me, makes me a better writer, and always finds my dangling modifiers. There are no words to express how grateful I am for her dedication, skill, and support. Thanks to Greg Erlandson, whose idea this book was, and to Bert Ghezzi, who initially brought it to my attention. Immense gratitude to Mike, Monica, and Fr. John for their generosity in sharing Harry's story (these are not their real names, and some details have been changed). To my husband, Tom, for his steadfast love, support, proofreading skills, and weekend cooking. To my daughters for their patience, sweetness, and trips to the library. Thanks to Danae and Johnna for everything, and to Marci for the inter-library loans she hunted down. As always, thanks to Fr. Joe Taphorn. And thank you to every bookseller everywhere who has ever sold an old treasure for a penny-plus-shipping.

I'm grateful to the many biographers whose in-depth books provided me with meat and muscle, which I have necessarily had to whittle down to bare bones. I wish I could give each of the subjects in these pages their own tome.

I researched primary sources if possible, but this is not a scholarly work, or an exhaustive exploration of the subjects. It is merely an abbreviated version of these conversions, fuller treatment of which can be found in the longer works I used for research. Please see the endnotes for ideas for further reading.

A final note: in several cases, I refer to the administration of "last rites" without specifying whether that included confession, Holy Communion (Viaticum), or anointing of the sick. I have retained the term "last rites" when sources used it, since in those cases it is impossible to know every detail of what transpired.

Additional Works Consulted

Rebecca Fraser, *The Story of Britain From the Romans to the Present: A Narrative History* (New York: W.W. Norton and Co., 2003).

David Starkey, *Monarchy,* Granada Video, 2004.

Frank Harris, *Oscar Wilde, His Life and Confessions, Vol. I and Vol. II* (Gutenberg).

Paul Glynn, *The Healing Fire of Christ* (San Francisco, CA: Ignatius Press, 2003).

James Newton, *Uncommon Friends: Life with Thomas Edison, Henry Ford, Harvey Firestone, Alexis Carrel and Charles Lindburgh* (Orlando, FL: Harcourt, 1987).

Holly Stevens, editor, *Letters of Wallace Stevens* (Berkeley, CA: University of California Press, 1981).

Joan Richardson, *Wallace Stevens: The Early Years, 1879–1923* (New York: Beech Tree Books, 1986).

Kenneth Clark, *The Other Half: A Self-Portrait* (New York: Harper & Row, 1977).

Kenneth Clark, *Civilisation: A Personal View* (New York: Harper & Row, 1969).

Claude Williamson, O.S.C., editor, *Great Catholics* (New York: The Macmillan Company, 1945).

Robert Ross, *Aubrey Beardsley*, http://www.gutenberg.org/files/33347/33347-h/33347-h.htm.

Thomas C. Reeves, *America's Bishop: The Life and Times of Fulton J. Sheen* (San Francisco, CA: Encounter Books, 2001).

"Death of a Journalist": http://archive.catholicherald.co.uk/article/12th-january-1940/10/death-of-a-journalist-i.

"Will Join Catholic Church, Broun Says": http://news.google.com/newspapers?nid=1955&dat=19390523&id=6lshAAAAIBAJ&sjid=EYgFAAAAIBAJ&pg=5583,4654757.

"My Years With Roald," by Elizabeth Day, about Felicity Crosland (http://www.guardian.co.uk/books/2008/nov/09/felicity-dahl-roald).

EWTN interview clip with Mother Dolores: http://www.youtube.com/watch?v=IvpmywFyoow.

Maria Cooper Janis, *Gary Cooper, Off Camera, A Daughter Remembers* (New York: Harry N. Abrams, Inc., 1999).

About the Author

Karen Edmisten is a convert to Catholicism and the author of several books, including *After Miscarriage: A Catholic Woman's Companion to Healing and Hope*. She has written for numerous publications and is a regular guest on Catholic radio. She blogs about faith, conversion, family, and life at karenedmisten.blogspot.com.